2⁵⁰

CORPORATE
EXECUTIONS

CORPORATE EXECUTIONS

The Ugly Truth About Layoffs—How Corporate Greed Is Shattering Lives, Companies, and Communities

Alan Downs

American Management Association

New York • Atlanta • Boston • Chicago • Kansas City • San Francisco • Washington, D. C.
Brussels • Mexico City • Tokyo • Toronto

This book is available at a special
discount when ordered in bulk quantities.
For information, contact Special Sales Department,
AMACOM, a division of American Management Association,
135 West 50th Street, New York, NY 10020.

Library of Congress Cataloging-in-Publication Data

Downs, Alan.
    Corporate executions : the ugly truth about layoffs—how corporate greed is
shattering lives, companies, and communities / Alan Downs.
    p.   cm.
    Includes bibliographical references and index.
    ISBN 0-8144-0307-7
    1. Layoff systems.   2. Downsizing of organizations.   3. Hours of
labor.   I. Title.
    HD5708.5.D69   1995
    331.25—dc20   95-20455
                                                                      CIP

Printing number

10   9   8   7   6   5   4   3   2   1

To
**Jason, Kevin, Timothy, David, Caleb, Chris,
Daniel, Colin, Connor,** and **Katherine.**
May they grow up to work in a world where
layoffs are an oddity of the past.

Contents

Preface

This book is an exposé of layoffs. For more than a decade, corporate America has been conducting an experiment: the cyclical purging of human assets. Throughout this period, every corporate employee has, without his or her consent, participated in a trial-and-error attempt to cut costs and increase profits. The data from this human experiment are now rolling in, and the results aren't good. A layoff carries an enormous cost, inflicts untold casualties, and yields only mediocre financial returns. Despite the evidence, the layoff experiment has moved from the realm of hypothesis to accepted truth. This version of corporate "truth," neither factual nor humane, has spread like dogma, first throughout American businesses and now to the rest of the world.

This book reveals the truth about the layoff experiment and its results. It offers example after example of impaired organizations that discovered layoffs only worsened their situation. Moreover, layoffs place tremendous stress and overwork on managers and take a toll on surviving employees and worker morale.

Communities also take a hard hit during a layoff. Decreased tax revenue and falling retail sales all snowball, creating a downward economic trend that ultimately is borne by all those who remain employed. Churches and schools must downsize or even close in response to diminished attendance and funds, further weakening the bonds of community. Families are pushed to the limit as they try to accommodate the loss of a paycheck with the least amount of devastation.

This book began with an unexpected phone call from my sister, Camille. When the call came, I was busily cleaning off my cluttered desk in preparation for a week's vacation. My sister and brother-in-law were flying out from Louisiana to San Francisco to join me for a week's vacation in a house we had rented on a secluded part of the northern California coast. All of us were anticipating a time apart, with no schedules, no phones, no television, and no work. I was escaping a hectic consulting practice, my sister was vacationing from her corporate management job, and her husband was leaving behind his music store for the first time in almost five years. We all agreed that for one glorious week, the pounding of the surf against the rocks would be our only metric of time.

The voice on the line I immediately recognized as that of my sister. Nervously she explained to me that, yes, mhh, they would still be coming, then paused before dropping the bombshell. Haltingly she told me what she still couldn't believe herself: She had been laid off. Laid off? How had that happened? Only a few months ago she had been awarded her company's Supervisor of the Year award. She had been flown to Dallas and treated to a night on the town in a chauffeured limousine. Now, weeks later, they were laying her off?

Actually, I knew all too well what had happened. Earlier in my career, I had been a layoff specialist for several large companies. I was the one who birthed the layoff from design table to execution. I was the one who sat in meeting after meeting with company managers discussing each name that would go. And for a while, I believed in the myth that a layoff was a necessary tool for managing a successful business.

One year prior to my sister's layoff, I had begun to see a disturbing trend in the companies with which I worked: Even after significant layoffs, these companies weren't doing so well. In fact, many were doing worse, *much worse*. What was going wrong? Were these companies in such bad shape to begin with that layoffs didn't make a difference? Maybe they weren't cutting deep enough. Or maybe they had cut too deep.

As I began to talk with my colleagues who worked with other companies as internal and external layoff consultants, I discovered they too had some mounting reservations. All of the published research I could get my hands on was also questioning the utility of layoffs. Try as I might, I found little beyond mere philosophic dogma and hopeful speculation to suggest layoffs really worked—and everything pointed in the direction that layoffs were as dangerous as the sickness they were supposed to cure. After mulling over the implications, I had a change of perspective about the efficacy of layoffs.

This book is the culmination of my travels among many organizations that have found even the best designed layoff to be a very bitter pill. From the personal experience of my sister to the cyclical demise of organizations that lay off, I show how layoffs are utterly destructive of everything they are mistakenly thought to fix. I give examples of numerous organizations, large and small, that have turned to the layoff doctors for help in time of crisis, only to find themselves in a hopeless cycle of binge-and-purge staffing while the company's health continues to fail.

In addition to discussing the disastrous costs of a layoff, this book presents some solutions for managing and reducing personnel costs *without* layoffs—for example, reducing hours worked and making changes in vacation liability and payroll. For a more proactive approach, I set out strategic planning methods for avoiding a layoff, and I discuss in detail the value of just-in-time human resources planning. To show that these planning methods work, I provide examples of companies that have used them and successfully avoided massive layoffs, even in difficult times.

In the last chapter, I look at the obsolete social contract of employment that is in effect today and the need to create a new contract with terms that are workable for both management and employees. This new contract will redefine the concept of employment and how workers relate to organizations. It removes the corporation from the protective parental role it has assumed over the past century and creates a negotiated relationship between employer and employee.

I have been touched by many American workers who were willing to sit and relate the painful transitions a layoff brings. I have heard from corporate managers who are weary and burned out from repeated downsizings, as well as members of the silent crowds who were forced to find new work at jobs that often pay less and offer little challenge. Their stories fill these pages. Their layoffs are the plot that has been hidden behind the well-intentioned clamor of corporate management to regain American industrial superiority. The collective drama lists millions of characters, each of whom deserves that the story be told in its entirety.

If layoffs truly were the cure for today's business, there would be no story here. They would still be painful—though necessary and prudent. But layoffs are not the cure, and the twisted carnage of human dignity and squandered corporate assets left in the layoff wake must be brought into the light of public inquiry and debate. I hope this book initiates just such a meaningful discussion and a search for change.

Acknowledgments

No book is ever written alone. The list of those who contributed in word and concept to this book is long and treasured. To all those who took the time to share their stories and relive often painful memories, I am deeply grateful.

I am indebted to my sister, Camille Stogner, for her contributions in both written word (Chapters 8 and 9) and moral support. Without her and the support of her husband, Jerry, and son, Colin, this book would be missing a vital perspective. Camille and I both thank our parents for a lifetime of unswerving support and love.

I have worked with many colleagues over the years, but none has influenced my own thinking and writing as much as Fredericka MacKenzie. Her insightful challenges and helpful guidance grace much of what is written here.

Special thanks go to W. Ray Smith and Steven Piersanti, who kept me on a steady diet of articles on layoffs and the plight of American workers. My hope is that this book will multiply their generous contribution of ideas and a shared love for the written word.

The process of writing and publishing this work were greatly enhanced by my agent, Julie Castiglia, and my friend and publishing adviser, Blanche Brann. I am indebted to the staff of AMACOM and my editor, Adrienne Hickey, for their willingness to listen to my ideas and publish them.

Finally, this book would have never materialized had it not been for Kevin Sloan. His constant encouragement and support kept me writing. His comments and countless reviews of the manuscript helped me over many hurdles, and for this help, I am deeply grateful.

Part One

The Jury Is In: Evidence and Verdict on Layoffs

Since the early 1980s, the forces of technological change have pushed American corporations into a newly formed, fiercely competitive global marketplace. No longer is it enough for organizations to produce for the brand-loyal American consumer; now they have to do so with the highest possible quality, the lowest price, and the most efficient distribution channels—and do all of this better than a host of competitors. Competition, however, isn't exactly being met on a level playing field. All too often the competitors are from countries where labor costs a fraction of what it is in the United States, taxes are lower (and there may even be government subsidies), industry regulations are minimal or nonexistent, and there are no labor unions with which to haggle. U.S. companies must manage all this *and* answer to a troop of Wall Street warriors who are ever vigilant to attack any management that fails to deliver expected earnings.

The preferred solution to this industrial dilemma has been to cut operating expenses. Cut, gouge, rip, and lay off until the numbers look right. It has been a very bitter pill, but one that was prescribed with the best of intentions. Unfortunately, the side effects of this pseudo-cure have turned out to be more disastrous than the disease.

Fifteen years of continually increasing layoffs have created a sizable bank of data and experience that show layoffs to be a less than effective means of dealing with the opposing forces of market competition and hungry shareholders. What originally appeared to be a cost-saving measure turns out to be a very expense prop for earnings.

1
The Truth About Layoffs

Lots of folks confuse bad management with destiny.

Kin Hubbard (1868–1930),
American humorist and journalist

Time was that when there was a layoff, the evening news showed streams of poor second- and third-generation coal miners trudging out of the gate of a dismally gray mine in Appalachia. Or maybe angry automotive workers were shaking their fists at starched white-shirts hiding inside industrial temples of steel and smokestacks. Perhaps foreign-born garment workers were leaving for the last time an old warehouse in some long-since-faded area of town. Whatever the scene, it was the kind that well-meaning parents used to prod their offspring into going to college and "making something" of themselves, "so this won't happen to you."

Times have changed.

Layoffs permeate all ranks of American business. The American Management Association found that in 1994, two-thirds of all workers who were laid off were college-educated, salaried employees. A college degree, a corner office, an officer title, years of seniority—nothing can vaccinate the worker from the grip of this plague. It has swept through every willing host in our society: large corporations, small partnerships, government agencies, universities and public school systems, and nonprofit organizations. Shedding workers has become fashionably strategic in almost every sector of American business.

The layoff fad of the past fifteen years began with companies that were trying to stop a decline in earnings, but it has now become popular to lay off employees even when things are going well. A recent headline from the *Pittsburgh Post-Gazette* read: WESTINGHOUSE REPORTS FIRST PROFIT SINCE 1990, LAYS OFF 1,200. Or Bank of America, which is recording record-breaking profits among banking institutions, has laid off 12,000 employees. These and countless other corporations are now using layoffs as a preemptive measure to ensure that profits continue to grow. One top executive described layoffs as "an operational hedge against unforeseen changes in the economic climate."

Many business leaders have blamed the layoffs of the past on a weak economy. Yet when the economy improved in 1994 and created 3 million new jobs, layoffs continued at a pace that was only slightly below that of the year before: 500,000 workers lost their jobs in announced layoffs. Despite the lowest unemployment rate in years, polls show Americans to be cautious and even fearful of their livelihoods, even those who have big, financially secure positions. Is it any wonder? Unexpected layoffs have become a way of life. On average, newly created jobs pay far less than those that have disappeared, and all wages, after adjusting for inflation, have risen only marginally since the mid-1970s.

Yet corporate gurus say we must cut back if American business is to grow! This widely accepted belief turns out to be not entirely true. Consider this scenario: A company's revenues drop, say, $1 million because of a temporary decline in sales, and managers must now decide how much to cut labor costs or how much to let profits fall. The company could cut labor costs and drop profits by an equal amount. Or it could leave the payroll intact and force shareholders to bear the brunt of the downturn. What have most American companies been doing? Maintaining profits by cutting jobs. When an American company's output falls by $1, the income of workers tends to decline 48 cents.

But there is another way: allowing the company's profits to fluctuate realistically with a decline in output, so there is less need to lay off workers. Passing losses as well as gains on to shareholders is healthier in the long run for the company and the economy.

A company that endures a layoff mercilessly bleeds critical personnel. It staggers from the loss of talent, knowledge, and morale for months, even years, after a layoff. The loss of productivity after a layoff is profound. Not only does the company lose needed employees; it loses customers. Layoffs destroy consumer confidence, and that causes the economy to stagnate.

History shows that a reduction in shareholder dividends does not have the same effect. Most investors dependent on dividend income are high-income individuals and institutions that own assets. When dividends decrease, they can—and apparently do—liquidate those assets in order to maintain their previous spending level.

The two countries where the workers' share of productivity fluctuations is lowest, Japan and Italy, also have the most stable economies. Countries experiencing the deepest recessions since 1988—Britain, Canada, and the United States—are also the countries most likely to lay off workers in a downturn. Layoffs, it seems, have become the bane of American corporations and the economy.

The Fitness Fiasco

I learned how common layoffs have become at the most unexpected of places: the gym. Although I try to keep my daily gym time free of such profundities, this one invaded my Zen hour like Attilla in pursuit. I learned long ago that the gym was a corporate necessity for me. I had to take an hour or so a day for myself. Since I had a boss who was prone to walking into my office at 5 P.M. with an hour or two of work to discuss, I began working out at 6 A.M. so nothing could interfere—or so I thought.

The first time I noticed a change was one winter morning when I stumbled into the locker room in my usual morning stupor and noticed Walter wasn't at the front desk. Walter, a weekday morning fixture there for as many years as I could remember, had been laid off.

As time went on, I began to notice other changes. The gym equipment, which inevitably breaks down, seemed to stay unrepaired for months at a time; the showers had started to reek with an odor that was reminiscent of my high school locker room; and the hot water heater seemed to be broken, until the front desk person walked inside a closet and flipped a miraculous little switch that fixed it—*after* I had finished. To top it all off, Manny, the retired schoolteacher who operated a small juice and coffee bar in the front corner of the main room, had also been let go. Where else could I go for breakfast on the fly?

The day I arrived at my usual hour and stood for fifteen minutes outside the locked doors in clothes that were barely more than pajamas, with my suit and starched shirt slung over my shoulders, was the day I decided I'd had enough. I returned to the gym at lunch in order to catch the manager during his workday.

When I arrived, he greeted me at the door and showed me to his office with an air of routine that let me know I hadn't been the only one to complain. Once inside, we commenced with the small talk that usually precedes a tense conversation. When I mentioned that I worked in human resources, his eyes lit up, and he reached inside the side drawer of his desk. "Ah," he said. "Then you'll understand what we're trying to do here."

With that he produced a nicely drawn diagram labeled "Change Model." It showed the six full and part-time positions at the gym, with lots of arrows showing what would happen to them. He explained that there was no need for a full-time front desk attendant like Walter under the new model. And the night-time cleaning staff had been laid off because with the new configuration, the staff would clean the locker rooms in the course of the day. Finally, he quickly dismissed my complaint about losing Manny and the coffee bar with a furrowed brow and frown: "You know, Manny never made a dime for the gym." All of these changes, including laying off Manny, were necessary to keep the gym profitable given the proliferation of competing gyms, he said.

I left in disgust. What kind of corporate fantasy were these muscle heads playing anyway? After all, it was just a gym. The gym had operated for years the old way, and, as far as I could tell, membership was at its highest level ever. It looked to me as if they had taken something that worked and broken it in the name of fixing it. Just maybe it was to wring a few more pennies out of a pregnant cash cow.

I returned that afternoon to my office, where for the past

several years, I had been focused on orchestrating corporate restructures and layoffs. I too had drawn many "change models" and explained to corporate executives why and how employees would do more with less. That's probably why the whole gym experience angered me so much. It was as if my own medicine had come back to poison that one hour of the day that was uniquely mine.

I learned in a very real and personal way that layoffs have become a fixture in business, no matter how big or small, bureaucratic or entrepreneurial. Layoffs are no longer the sole property of large industrial management. Businesses of all configurations are using the layoff cleaver to trim the fat from the employee ranks.

The fact that the gym manager used the word *layoff*, to describe what was happening, implied "it was unavoidable" and "the business could not afford to pay those employeees." Neither was true in this situation, nor, as it turns out, in most layoffs. Had he said *fired* or *let go*, I might have challenged his decision with my own observations of those employees' performance.

Within two years after the gym's "restructuring," the membership had dwindled so much that it closed its doors. Now I can't speak for all the members, but my gym buddies and I left because of the lack of service that happened *after* the restructuring and layoff. The little things—opening the doors on time, repairing the equipment, straightening the weight room, providing plenty of clean towels and ample hot water, a locker room that looks and smells clean—stopped happening. These things are important to the gym customers. They represent the extra effort that committed and motivated employees give to a business that pushes it ahead of the competition. After the layoff, it was clear that the employees had lost their motivation to do anything more than just what was required.

This story of the gym's demise captures the essence of this book. Mounting evidence—solid business results—suggests that a layoff creates a downward spiral that can boost financial results in the short term but also creates a need for multiple, successive layoffs to maintain those results. Like an anorexia of the organization, it begins depleting the organization of its fat, then its muscle, and finally its brain power. This process will continue until a wiser management team intervenes and stops the addictive cycle.

The Reasons Behind Layoffs

Why did this practice of mass firings begin, and how is it that layoffs have been accepted as an effective means to business restructuring? Perhaps the best way to understand this is to imagine yourself sitting in a room, a room to which you have been unexpectedly summoned to be told that you are now laid off. I'll take the position I occupied for literally hundreds of layoff meetings and tell you the story I told those fated employees about why their paychecks have been revoked. Here are several versions of the same message:

The Lean-and-Mean Story

"The business climate these days has become enormously more competitive. Global markets have contributed new competitors that can offer goods and services at a much lower cost than American producers. For the American organization to be competitive, it must remain lean and trim costs wherever possible. That means we must retain only those jobs that are essential to the business. Your job, unfortunately, is not essential and has been eliminated."

The Strategic Flexibility Story

"The rapid pace of technological change continues to affect our organization. Products we made five years ago are now obsolete. The key to our company's survival is being able to keep up with this ever-increasing rate of change. This means continually reconfiguring our organization in order to position ourselves with these changes and to be a future leader in the marketplace. As a result, we have decided to discontinue the product you produce and go with a new technology. Your job no longer exists."

The "Learning Organization" Story

"The key to success in today's world is continual learning and process improvement. The minute we stop moving forward, learning and using new technologies, we start moving backward. Continuous learning means that everyone in the organization must stay abreast of changes in their field and keep their skills updated. Unfortunately, in your case, the job has changed dramatically in the past few years. We now need someone with skills and degrees you do not possess. Therefore, we are laying you off."

The Mystical Management Story
[used to lay off managers]

"Leadership is a highly prized asset around here. We believe strongly in the motto, 'Lead, follow, or get out of the way.' We expect all members of our management team to be leaders. They must have that extra something that inspires their people to new heights of performance and increases commitment to the company. We depend on our managers to supply the pizzazz that makes this company so special. Sometimes a particular combination of a manager and employees just never seems to develop this kind of rapport. I'm afraid this is the case in your situation, and we don't see much chance for change. We think it would be advisable that you consider the package we are offering you and to leave the company rather than have your career damaged by the consequences that could occur down the road."

The "We're Out of Money" Story

"As you may know, the company's performance has not been great recently. We are now at the point where there just aren't enough funds to keep all of our emplolyees on the payroll. Since I have been told to eliminate 10 percent of my employees, I have decided that your job is the one that we will have to do without. I'm sorry, but I have no other choice but to lay you off."

The Eye on the Prize Story

"As a company, we committed at the beginning of this fiscal year to reach some very challenging goals. We've worked hard all year and accomplished much, but not quite enough to meet our commitments. As the year draws to a close, it has become clear that the only way we will make our goal is to reduce expenses. Each manager has agreed to reduce the staff by one. Because you have the least seniority on staff, your job has been eliminated."

Companies have legitimate reasons for dropping massive numbers of employees from their ranks. Global competition, the need to loosen hierarchies, rapid technological change, cost cutting, aggressive financial expectations of investors, and obsolete workforces are just some of the ailments that plague today's businesses. These are serious concerns—concerns that, if left untreated, can be terminal to the organization. As many of the tried and true organizations of the past fall prey to these new corporate viruses of the twenty-first century, others are grasping for a cure. Many think a layoff is just such a cure, and they religiously hold to the ritual of slimming the corporation as the only path back to health.

Certainly layoffs relieve some of these more painful symptoms. The payroll, for example, is usually the highest operating expense of a company. Reducing the largest number yields the greatest savings. A layoff can also help with the problem of obsolete workers. Laying off those whose skills aren't up to par makes room for a new crop of employees whose abilities are more current. In addition, a layoff can make a reorganization much easier on management. Anyone who has managed a group through a restructuring will testify that hiring an employee into a newly created position is much easier than trying to coddle existing employees so they accept the new. As far as those demanding investors go, a layoff shows management's strong commitment to do whatever it takes to reduce expenses. Accordingly, Wall Street often sends a strong vote of confidence to such action by raising the stock price significantly.

A number of companies have used a layoff to save their corporate hides. IBM, Digital Equipment Corporation, Macy's, Continental Airlines, and General Motors have boosted their quarterly earnings during times of tremendous financial difficulty by slashing the payroll. They effectively averted a financial crisis that would have surely meant disaster had they not dramatically cut their expenses. The layoffs bought them time.

The rest of American business, seeking relief from this onslaught of trouble, has also slimmed its ranks by the millions.

Between 1980 and 1993, the employment rosters of the Forbes 500 companies fell by 10 percent, to 20.2 million workers. And for all employers, large and small, the number of workers laid off during this same period totals more than 8 million—the equivalent of laying off the entire city of New York or unemploying all of the self-employed people in the United States at the 1990 census.

This exercise in trimming wasn't just limited to the big guys, either. Right Associates, a consulting firm, found that during the 1980s, 45 percent of those companies with 500 to 1,000 employees and 56 percent of those with 1,000 to 5,000 employees conducted layoffs. Year after year, during recession and, paradoxically, growth periods, the numbers get bigger. Four times as many employees were laid off in 1991 as in 1989, and the total for 1994 is equal to what it was in 1993. In September 1993 alone, businesses were slashing jobs at the incredible rate of 2,000 a day. And those figures reflect only larger corporations that announced layoffs. Some experts estimate that the actual numbers could be twice as high.

But despite the popularity of this "solution," not all is well with those who have swallowed the bitter layoff pill. The evidence that is emerging now questions the long-term efficacy of this "miracle" cure. Do layoffs really cure the disease or simply borrow from the future of the organization? By solving today's crisis, do they create a debt that can choke the life out of the organization in the long term? The data confirm that layoffs most often appear to alleviate only today's corporate symptoms. In reality, they destroy the future health of the organization.

The Evidence Against Layoffs

Some of the strongest evidence condemning layoffs comes from Wyatt and Co., one of the most respected organizational survey firms in the country. A survey of 1,005 corporations that had recently participated in a downsizing program found the following.

* Only one-third said that profits increased as much as they had expected after the layoff.

▪ Fewer than half said that their cuts had reduced expenses as much as expected over time—an understandable result, considering that four out of five of these same managers reported rehiring for the positions that were laid off.
▪ Only a small minority reported a satisfactory increase in shareholders' return on investment as a result of the layoff.

As if those results weren't eye-opening enough, Wyatt and Co. released a follow-up study a year later that extended these earlier findings and prompted editorials in both *The Wall Street Journal* and *Money*. In this study, 531 large corporations were surveyed, and more than three-quarters reported having cut their payrolls. Of those, 85 percent sought higher profits from the layoff, but only 46 percent saw any measurable increase. Fifty-eight percent of this same group sought higher productivity, but only 34 percent reported even a slight increase. Sixty-one percent wanted an improvement in customer service, but only 31 percent achieved it. And as in other studies, within one year following the cuts, more than half of the companies had refilled the laid-off positions.

Wyatt and Co. is not the only corporate research organization with such bleak findings. A series of studies conducted by the American Management Association (AMA) concluded that two words sum up the ineffectiveness of layoffs: *poor management*. First, they found that long-range planning before a layoff was the exception, not the rule. Why aren't they planning? Executives often view future costs to be predictable and future revenues as less so. Thus, they focus on cost reduction rather than increasing revenues. So in a twisted way, a layoff becomes a plan for the future—a way to reduce the only sure thing about the future: costs.

One of the AMA studies, a survey of 547 companies that had downsized between 1986 and 1992, found that only a minority of these companies (43.5 percent) actually improved operating profits. These statistics were confirmed in a separate study by Kenneth De Meuse at the University of Wisconsin, who found that profits actually declined faster *after* the layoff.

Additional AMA research has found that 60 percent of the companies that laid off employees in 1992 also laid off employees in 1993. In a 1994 AMA study, two-thirds of the companies that laid off also reported hiring new employees in other areas. Now when you combine this with the Wyatt and Co. finding that most laid-off positions are refilled within two years, a binge-and-purge picture begins to emerge. With a watchful eye to quarterly results, company management opens and closes the hiring gate according to short-term financials, not long-term business needs. Staff up when things look good, in other words, and lay off when they start to slip. Moreover, this cycle that perpetuates and feeds itself is a very expensive process. Dow Chemical estimates that the cost of rehiring a single technical or managerial employee is as much as $50,000.

This addictive cycle has ravaged what once was one of America's most revered companies, Eastman Kodak. The photography giant began its foray into restructures and layoffs back in 1985 and since then has restructured *five times*. The total bill? More than $2.1 billion and 12,000 jobs. And here's what it got for all that effort: halved profit margins, a less than desirable stock price, and total revenues that aren't much larger than before they fell into the restructuring black hole.

We have been looking only at the macro trends—the big picture. As always with collective data, a company may not exactly match the averaged, overall trend. That is, not every company that lays off employees does so with spurious reasoning, and a few organizations do find that a layoff actually achieves their goals. Although many of these figures are self-reported and the success figures probably less than actually given, nonetheless some companies have used the layoff successfully. Still, what is in question is not that layoffs can sometimes and in some cases be effective. Rather, it is the wholesale acceptance of layoffs as a panacea for what ails corporations in the nineties that is highly suspect. Layoffs emerge as a risky, painful, and inhumane form of management that only in the worst cases can resuscitate a dying organization. Using it to treat the quarterly stubbed toe is worse than doing nothing at all.

So Why Is It the Change Tactic of Choice?

Wall Street

Layoffs have become the change tactic of choice for several compelling reasons, not the least of which is the effectiveness of a layoff on Wall Street (Exhibit 1). How does an average increase in stock price of 8 percent grab you? When the chips are down and the big boss is watching, it can look really good. Investors often applaud the news of a layoff as a sign of a corporate turnaround. The payroll is a large, ongoing liability to the balance sheet, and investors are titillated by anything that reduces it.

Some business and industry leaders have begun to acknowledge the hand of Wall Street in initiating layoffs. Robert Reich, U.S. secretary of labor, has chided bankers and financial analysis for their wholehearted support of layoffs. He noted, "The typical upturn in stock prices immediately upon announcement of a layoff is based more on a collective anticipation by investors that other investors will respond positively to the same news, than it is on any change in the fundamentals."

Exhibit 1. Gain in stock price after a layoff for selected U.S. companies.

Company	Number of Employees Laid Off	Date Layoff Was Announced	Rise in Stock Price by December 27, 1993
Boeing	21,000	February 18, 1993	31%
IBM	60,000	July 27, 1993	30%
Procter and Gamble	13,000	July 15, 1993	13%
Sears Roebuck	50,000	January 25, 1993	3%
United Technologies	10,500	January 26, 1993	30%

Yet like the other pseudo-benefits of a layoff, any upturn in stock price is short-lived. A Mitchell & Co. study of sixteen major firms that cut more than 10 percent of their workforce between 1982 and 1988 found that although Wall Street initially applauded the cuts with higher stock prices, two years later ten of the sixteen stocks were trading below the stock market by 17 to 48 percent. Worse, twelve of these companies were trading below comparable firms in their industries.

Employee Performance

Another reason for the popularity of layoffs lies in what I like to call *mass performance management.* No hard numbers can capture this aspect yet it is often a significant factor among executives who are driving the layoff. They see it as a quick way to purge the organization of those who are perceived as not pulling their weight. By creating an environment of fear, executives hope to scare employees into working harder.

Picture this situation: Things have been going steadily downhill for several years, and morale is in the basement. Whining and watching your back have replaced any semblance of risk taking and entrepreneurial management. As a senior executive, you realize this is the perfect opportunity to dump the worst naysayers while sending to the rest a strong message of warning whose meaning is unmistakable. No matter how it is phrased—"The bar has been raised," "We're pushing the needle around here," "Nothing short of excellence"—whatever the words or catchphrases, when combined with a layoff it is a strong and fearful method of managing employee performance.

Publicity

At first glance it might appear that the publicity from a layoff would be bad for business. But in a surprising number of cases, it can actually be beneficial. Nothing else gets a company's name in the paper more quickly than an announcement of a layoff. During times when the company's tax payments to the local governments are negotiated, that kind of press can have a favorable effect. The same goes for office rent and bank loans. If the company is a major employer in the community, everyone will suffer if too many people lose their jobs, and community leaders will do whatever they can to avert such a crisis. Not a few companies operate under highly favorable conditions because of threats to have another layoff.

Executives Look Busy

The most attractive aspect of a layoff is that it is an organizational change with clear, predictable consequences: Reducing the payroll lowers expenses. With any other kind of executive action, like process improvement or total quality, the consequences are not nearly as clear or immediate. Months, maybe even years, may pass before those improvements make any noticeable difference in the basic financials. And when they finally have a positive effect, the time and distance between the actual decision and the result make it very difficult for a specific person to claim the credit for the accomplishment. A layoff, on the other hand, can be decided and announced by a senior executive and within a very short time period that same executive can claim credit for a reduction in expenses. When things are going badly, being able to look decisive and to take credit for "moving in the right direction" is invaluable to a management career on thin ice.

So when you put it all together—the upturn in stock price, the immediate reduction in operating costs, the chance to fire the poor performers, the free publicity, and the opportunity to look decisive—that layoffs have increased exponentially year after year is no wonder. For corporate management, investors, and a working public that fixate on short-term, quarterly results, the quick payback from a layoff is hard to deny.

The Downside

Before we cheer too loudly, there is one more aspect of the layoff I haven't touched on: the millions of lives and careers that have been virtually destroyed by its ravages.

Imagine what it must have been like to work for the Grand Rapids, Michigan, medical collection agency that was recently sold to its leading competitor. When this merger was announced to the employees by the now former owner, he also made a few more shocking announcements. To start off, he read a list of middle managers who would not be retained by the new owners. This was the first time these people had heard they were being laid off, and the announcement was made in front of all the employees while they stood listening in the parking lot. Then he proceeded to inform the employees who were staying on that since the new owners did not provide health insurance coverage, they were, as of that very moment, no longer covered. Finally, he warned that the new management would be working to streamline operations, and more cuts would inevitably occur. Those who still had a job, he proclaimed, should be thankful.

Not every layoff is so brutally cold, but the toll on employees is always the same. The loss of self-confidence can be devastating when a job is unexpectedly and thanklessly jerked away. According to many who have been through it, some more than once, the emotional and psychological cost is immeasurable—not to mention the hole a layoff can poke in an otherwise credential-rich and progressive resumé.

Bouncing Back

"If I were laid off," you might be thinking, "it would be tough, but eventually I'd get another job and get on with my life." Well, maybe not. Consider what has happened to the unemployed: In the 1970s, 11 percent of the unemployed were out of work for six months or more; in the 1980s, it was 15 percent; and so far in the 1990s, it is 16 percent. In 1992 alone, that figure jumped above 20 percent, the highest level since the end of World War II. Of all those who have lost full-time work, more than half remain unemployed a year later or employed in jobs that pay less than 80 percent of their previous wages.

Bouncing back isn't easy. The median wage of reemployed workers declines on average 11.8 percent, with 25 percent of these workers losing health insurance benefits. If you are over age 40, have worked for the same company all your career, have had health problems, or have disabilities, the news is worse. What it boils down to is this: Most laid-off workers do eventually find other employment after several months of looking. Their new job, however, often pays less than their previous job, health care coverage is reduced, there may be fewer hours than full-time employment, and the challenges and opportunities for advancement may be fewer.

In the long run, a layoff is the cure that can kill. The side effects from this prescription can be more devastating to both company and employee than the original ailment. But before we place the blame for this catastrophe squarely in the hands of its executive keepers, it is important to realize that it sprang to popularity from public pressure—pressure from hungry investors, an impatient media, and demanding financiers, all of whom cheer the massacre onward. As a working public, we too have come to bless the layoff as painful but necessary. Regretfully, we have accepted the reasoning that corporate pruning is the precursor for growth.

Public Acceptance

The public acceptance of layoffs is of no small significance to their expanding use. Despite the fact that layoffs have flourished during some of the strongest economic growth years of the past three decades, we as a society have accepted mass firings as status quo. Historically, this has not always been the case. Until very recently, a layoff was viewed as a sign of poor and inadequate management. Companies would do whatever they could to avoid letting their employees go. It was the choice of last resort. Today, it is often the only option considered. Rather than firing management that creates the need for a layoff, some companies, as in the highly publicized case of Eastman Kodak, are firing senior executives who are unwilling to lay off employees.

The history behind the acceptance of this practice goes back to the Great Depression of the 1930s. From that time through the 1970s, a layoff was not a permanent firing but only a temporary stop in work—work that would resume as soon as the business improved. Laid-off workers were often given a small stipend while they waited to be called back. In those days, a layoff was actually more humane than a firing. It showed the employer's willingness and commitment to do whatever it could to get the employee back on the payroll. Today a layoff means a permanent termination of employment.

Some of this public acceptance of layoffs can be credited to American society's rigidly and widely held belief in a just world, the grandfather to the Protestant work ethic. That belief— everything happens for a just reason—dictates that those who were laid off probably deserved it. By holding on to this idea, we create the illusion of control and job security. Because I am a good employee and hard worker, I will never be laid off. The unfortunate reality is that employees rarely have any control over a layoff, and those who do lose their jobs suffer the effects of an undeserved black mark on their employment record.

Despite the fact that as a society we have accepted the practice of layoffs, it is society that pays dearly for them. A layoff does nothing to improve the worker's education or capacity to create wealth; it is merely a very expensive method of pushing work around from one worker to the next. Communities and social institutions like schools and churches are often ripped apart by a local employer's decision to lay off a portion of the community's workforce. Because local governments spend millions of dollars on the infrastructure necessary to support big business, they are hit hard by the sudden loss of tax base. The bills for wider streets, water and sewerage systems, power plants, and other public goods suddenly fall on the shoulders of a smaller, poorer citizenry. The price of a layoff goes well beyond the corporate balance sheet or employee bank account. Those fingers reach deep into the pockets of every one of us and exact a heavy toll.

Alternatives to Layoffs

Are there alternatives to layoffs for businesses that are fighting the battle of the payroll bulge? Absolutely. Some well-managed companies have been employing various techniques that have seen the company through crisis without having a mass layoff. Consider Dow Chemical, which abstained from a hiring indulgence even when business was booming. One of the primary reasons it shunned staffing up was to avoid the possibility of an eventual layoff. According to Dow's figures, laying off a manager can cost anywhere from $30,000 to $100,000 and sometimes even more. CEO Frank Popoff holds the strong conviction that "layoffs are horribly expensive and destructive of shareholder value." When earnings dropped to an overwhelming 62 percent between 1989 and 1991 the company didn't have to unload expensive employees. When business continued to lag in 1993–1994, Dow was able to reduce its payroll through attrition and by offering, not forcing, early retirement.

Other companies too have recently experienced tough times yet avoided a layoff. When 3M's net income dropped 12 percent, the company began making some major changes, but mass firings of employees were not among them. Hewlett-Packard, which has undergone significant changes in its structure since 1990, has handled unneeded employees through its internal "excess" program and by offering voluntary severance packages. The excess program boasts a high rate of placement of extra employees into other jobs in the company. Sometimes this program encompasses retraining, including even basic skills training, such as English as a second language or mathematics. Each of these companies has realized that the cost of a layoff in dollars and morale is too high a price to pay.

The time has come to question the basic assumpiton that layoffs are an acceptable tool for business success and growth. The data are in, and they don't support the widespread and indiscriminate use of layoffs of the past decade. We must take a hard look at a practice that is dreadfully painful—painful to management, employees, communities, investors, and company performance. Frank Lalli, editor of *Money* magazine, put it succinctly in the February 1992 issue: "Therefore, as often as not, downsizing announcements should be read as warnings to workers to run before they're pushed and as signals to investors to sell before the stock slumps. . . . It's a warning to workers and investors alike that small minds tend to think small."

Throughout the rest of this book, we will explore the many faces of a layoff, take a close look at the effects of a layoff, and offer some alternative solutions that successful companies are using instead of swinging the ax.

2

The Rise of Corporate Narcissism

It's a sin to lose money, a mortal sin. [*Statement made after the elimination of 10,500 jobs, one-third of Scott Paper's workforce.*]

Albert J. Dunlap, CEO, Scott Paper

Balancing the Corporate Triangle

David Packard could be called the "virtual" grandfather of America's high-tech industry. This tall, unassuming man now in his eighties cofounded the instrument and computer giant Hewlett-Packard well over half a century ago. His deliberate and values-centered management style has proved to be overwhelmingly successful for the company—and has also repeatedly won him a spot on the list of the richest people in America. When asked recently what he considered to be his most outstanding achievement, this once undersecretary of defense said it was his creation of the "HP way" of management. Equally at home in the corridors of corporate and government power or eating a sandwich with workers on the loading dock of one of HP's manufacturing facilities, he is a brilliant engineer and the consummate leader.

A number of years ago when I was a new employee of Hewlett-Packard, I heard David Packard speak about his personal philosophy of management. As the cornerstone of his talk, he drew a triangle with each of the three points accentuated. At each point he wrote one of the following labels: shareholders, management, and employees. This, he said, was the fundamental secret to successful management. Any good management decision is based on the best interests of each of these three corporate constituents, keeping the triangle balanced. A decision that undermines any one of these ultimately undermines the company's long-term success.

I have often thought about that balanced triangle. The nature of business in a free market system always dictates a certain amount of tension among management, shareholders, and employees. Yet that tension provides the checks and balances for any organization. When management dominates the triangle, as it did during the industrial revolution, or when employees dominate the triangle, as often happened in the post–labor movement, the organization suffers and may eventually succumb to its own vulnerability. The shareholder-management-employee tension, as uncomfortable as it may be at times, is critical to the healthy organization.

Evidence of this tension swirls around the corporate citizen every day, with each side of the triangle pulling against the other. For example, one senior manager described for *Esquire* magazine how management and boards of directors pull against one another; in his description of boards that overrule company management, he refers to the boards as "meat eating." As for management-employee tension, consider Carl Icahn, CEO of TWA, who privately referred to flight attendants as not being breadwinners and as "replaceable." The tension between management and hostile shareholders took center stage in the 1980s with the invention of "greenmail," a management tactic to deny shareholders dividends by paying large sums of money to would-be acquirers. By having adjacent and opposing interests, each of these three parties provides a counterforce for the self-interests of the other.

The Lopsided Triangle

Increasingly in the 1990s, it has become acceptable—in some circles, even desirable—for one member of this corporate trio to dominate the rest, destroying that critical balance. Shareholders scream for the company to increase profits, raise the stock price, and pay larger dividends—and they are increasingly getting their way. Management demands ever increasing compensation, exorbitant bonuses, and stock options for running the company for the shareholders—and they too are getting what they want. Employees often find themselves paying the price for this imbalance through repeated layoffs and overwork.

Today little is said when a CEO takes home many millions of dollars in compensation while simultaneously laying off thousands of workers. It happens almost daily. Consider these excerpts from two articles, which both appeared on March 11, 1994:

From the *Glen Falls Post-Star*

IBM Corp., as part of its goal to cut over 30,000 jobs this year, laid off 800 New York workers Thursday from its Large Scale Computing Division. . . .

IBM announced last July that it would trim its work force from 256,000 to 225,000 by 1994. The plan has resulted in the first IBM layoffs since the company was founded in 1914. . . .

"It's something we must do to stay competitive," spokesman Stephen Cole said.

From *The New York Times*

The chairman and chief executive of the IBM Corporation, Louis V. Gerstner, Jr., has earned $7.71 million in salary, bonuses and other cash compensation since he joined IBM in March.

Mr. Gerstner, 52, also received stock options that could be worth up to $38.2 million, IBM said in its annual proxy statement filed today with the SEC. . . .

He is to receive a total of $8.5 million for his first 12 months of service, a spokesman for IBM said.

Sometimes this imbalance of power becomes so great that the corporate triangle collapses. When shareholders and management pool their common self-interests, the organizing princi-ples of the corporation break down completely. This was the case in February 1991 at General Dynamics. Cold as it may have been in St. Louis on February 15, 1991—inside the General Dy-namics headquarters, it was nothing less than warm and cozy. That was the day the compensation committee of the board of directors sat down to consider revising the compensation pack-age of its CEO, William Anders, and twenty-four other top exec-utives. When the meeting concluded, they had approved a package that feathered the nest of the executives and lined their own pockets as well. In the minds of those committee members, it was a stroke of good management: They were simply provid-ing incentive to company management to succeed, which would in turn increase the value of their own investments in the com-pany.

Under the approved plan, the executives would receive a bonus equal to their yearly salary if General Dynamics stock rose ten points, from $25.56 per share to $35.56, and stayed there for ten days. If the stock went up another ten points to $45.56 per share and stayed *there* for ten days, they would receive a bonus equal to twice their yearly salary, and so on until the plan expired in 1994.

Now, it is no small feat to raise the stock price of a defense contractor in a time of major defense cuts by a few points, much less ten. They needed something monumental—something that would grab the attention of the media and investors on Wall Street while also sweetening the bottom line by increasing the cash on hand. Somehow General Dynamics would have to look like a good investment for no fewer than ten days. So what do you suppose that Mr. Anders and those other executives did?

They announced a massive layoff of more than 12,000 of the company's 86,000 employees, cut spending in other areas, and froze the salaries of anyone below their ranks. By the end of the year, they had amassed $600 million in cash, which they prom-ised to spread among the shareholders, and earned themselves $18 million in bonuses as the stock price held to the $45.56 mark for the tenth day. Anders personally received more than $9 mil-lion in salary and bonuses.

When employees protested the payouts and the public decried the jobs-for-cash grab, the General Dynamics compensation committee suspended the plan, in exchange, giving Anders 160,000 shares of stock, thus cooling the bad publicity but continuing the benefits of the plan. By the end of 1992, Anders received a whopping $21 million in compensation for that year alone.

General Dynamics isn't alone in using these tactics. More and more companies are giving in to the demands of constituents whose interest and motivation have little to do with the long-term success of the company, the people who work there and actually *earn* the money, the suppliers whose livelihood may depend on the company, or even the customers. These constituents see the company solely as a tool for personal gain.

The Culture of Corporate Narcissism

How has this happened? How is it that corporate America has lost its critical balance and given in to the tyranny of whoever can grab the largest share of power? Among the number of factors that have contributed to this dilemma, including some very difficult economic recessions, increasing global competition, and the conversion of industry from manufacturing to service, the biggest is the creation and public acceptance of a *culture of narcissism* in business.

The culture of corporate narcissism says that anything is acceptable as long as it is legal and makes money. The idea that a company should be run according to David Packard's triangle, where shareholders earn a profit, successful management makes a good living, and employees have a secure and productive place to earn a paycheck, is quickly fading from the American business scene. The culture of corporate narcissism has but one objective: profit. Profit as the singular standard by which a company is managed and measured has become the accepted norm. Under the culture of corporate narcissism, it is perfectly acceptable to lay off thousands of workers, slash health care benefits, economically devastate communities, and pay management astronomical salaries, all for an increase in profit. To criticize these practices is to have the wag of the Wall Street finger with the retort, "That's just business."

Defenders of the culture of narcissism assert that there is nothing wrong with making a profit, and I must heartily agree. Profit, the cornerstone of capitalism, is not the great evil in narcissism; the problem is the sole fixation on profit, to the detriment of all other values. Everything is expendable in the pursuit of fulfilling self-interest.

But there is a different way. It is possible to manage a company according to multiple values, including profit and employee welfare. It is possible for management to succeed and reap the rewards for their accomplishments. It is possible for a company to have a community and family consciousness and still be on the cutting edge of success. Many companies have bucked the tide of corporate narcissism and managed to make a nice chunk of profit too. Unfortunately, the majority of American companies aren't willing to take this path.

Narcissism vs. Empowerment

But what about empowerment? Employee involvement? Teamwork? Aren't these management fads evidence of a higher-level, group-based value system? The gradual failure of many of these programs suggests otherwise. For the most part, these are simply good ideas that well-meaning human resources departments have pushed on organizations. If any of these ideas makes it to executive boardrooms, they are often accepted as good etiquette but not serious business strategy.

This is a corporate paradox of the 1990s: Organizational rhetoric revolves around teamwork, shared values, vision, total quality, and empowerment, but high-level executive decisions are often contrary to these principles. In fact, it is common for someone in the chain of command to discover that he or she can use these programs as a means for personal advancement. Subtly, the program moves from employee involvement to employee manipulation, a manifestation of the singular, self-interest value in the culture of narcissism.

Narcissism and Senior Executive Salaries

The culture of corporate narcissism often has its strongest influence among senior managers and boards of directors. No stronger example exists than in the pay of senior executives. From 1980 to 1995, senior executive pay increased a whopping 1,000 percent. These were the years scarred with the largest numbers of layoffs ever recorded, yet executives hauled in an unprecedented share. Trying to avoid getting caught with their hand in the compensation cookie jar, many of these executives received a significant share of their income through stock options and bonus plans, which are harder to track and don't appear on the annual report. Yet these are no crumbs, as evidenced by a *Fortune* magazine report that in 1993 the average senior executive's stock incentive plan was worth twenty-three times his or her base salary for the year. Even more shocking is the fact that of the Forbes 500 companies, the CEO's salary was 157 times the average worker's pay.

No doubt, many boards of directors would quickly assert that keeping a company profitable in today's business environment requires executives to make some difficult decisions, and that is why these executives are paid so handsomely. This assertion has little basis in fact. The same Fortune report found no relationship at all between the total compensation of the CEO and the return on investment to shareholders for the 100 companies for which data were reported.*

So if executives aren't paid for company performance, why the big paychecks? One shocking piece of data suggests at least part of the answer. Of the companies in the report, twenty-two announced plans to lay off large groups of employees during 1994. When we correlate the number of employees to be laid off with total CEO compensation, a much stronger and statistically significant relationship emerges (correlation = .31). Conclusion: CEOs who lay off large numbers of employees are paid more than those who don't (Exhibit 2).

*The statistical correlation is .07, indicating no detectable link between the two factors.

Exhibit 2.   Number of layoffs and CEO salary.

	Number of Layoffs	Percentage Return[a]	CEO Salary
IBM	85,000	−10.4	$15,252,000
AT&T	83,500	16.4	$4,830,000
GM	74,000	10.8	$2,444,000
Sears	50,000	16.4	$6,905,000
GTE	32,150	15.3	$2,750,000
Boeing	30,000	12.5	$4,795,000
NYNEX	22,000	10.1	$2,506,000
Eastman Kodak	20,000	9.2	$25,392,000
Martin Marietta	15,000	20.4	$4,424,000
du Pont	14,800	14.7	$1,979,000
Philip Morris	14,000	21	$5,069,000
Citicorp	13,000	11.8	$13,125,000
Procter & Gamble	13,000	25	$3,414,000
Xerox	12,500	14.4	$2,352,000
BankAmerica	12,000	25.1	$5,241,000
Aetna	11,800	11.4	$4,096,000
United Technologies	10,697	12.4	$3,052,000
GE	10,250	22.1	$9,805,000
McDonnel Douglas	10,200	11.1	$1,184,000
Bellsouth	10,200	13.5	$2,355,000
Ford	10,000	11	$5,501,000
TRW	10,000	14.9	$1,614,000
Pacific Telesis	10,000	17.2	$2,548,000

[a]Five-year annual return to shareholders.

In fact, the pay of many senior executives seems to have little to do with company performance. When William Agee resigned as the chief executive of Morrison Knudsen Corporation in early 1995, that company had recorded a loss of $114 million over the previous two years. During that time, Agee received $3.5 million in cash and other unspecified benefits. On leaving the company, his severance package was estimated to be between $1.5 million and $4.8 million by a compensation expert. Ironically, at the time of paying Agee his generous golden parachute, Morrison Knudsen laid off 277 workers with no severance pay.

Narcissism and the Board of Directors

Another related form of narcissism took a rise during the 1980s when leveraged buyouts and corporate takeovers drained company assets, artificially raised the stock price, and left the company to deal with the debt. This shareholder asset plundering was perfected by the likes of Michael Milken and Frank Lorenzo but is not the sole prerogative of corporate raiders. Increasingly, shareholder groups are demanding "special" dividends and the sale of corporate assets to generate earnings.

Shareholder pressure can reap generous rewards for those who hold even small percentages of a company's stock. Los Angeles financier Kirk Kerkorian, who currently owns 9 percent of Chrysler Corporation stock, wrote to the Chrysler board of directors strongly suggesting that they raise the dividend, repurchase stock, split the stock, and eliminate the "poison pill"—the antitakeover provisions triggered when a shareholder accumulates 10 percent of the company's stock. What did he get for his efforts? The board raised the dividend 60 percent and announced it would buy back $1 billion in stock, measures that boosted the price of the shares. That translates into payments of $12.8 million every three months to Kerkorian. Not a bad deal when you consider it raised his annual return on investment by just over $30 million.

The most common shareholder tactic is to pressure management to negotiate lower wages or lay off employees to generate a spike in earnings and higher dividend payments. When the board of directors at Eastman Kodak dumped its former CEO, Kay R. Whitmore, it wasn't because the company wasn't making money. They sacked the top boss because he refused to initiate a layoff in response to a downturn in revenues. Since then Kodak, under new CEO George Fisher, has announced layoffs of more than 10,000 employees and is predicting that 2,000 to 5,000 more will lose their jobs by 1997, leaving little doubt that Fisher has clearly heard his marching orders.

The Values Landslide

The culture of corporate narcissism represents a dramatic change in values. Employees, once seen as assets to be cultivated and protected, now are more like disposable units to be used, then discarded at will. This change in values was recently brought to light by a member of one of the most prominent San Francisco banking families, Claire Giannini, granddaughter of the founder of Bank of America, who was outraged.

In February 1993 the Bank of America, after laying off 28,930 workers, proudly announced what was believed to be the highest profit for any banking institution *in history*, $1.5 billion. Its CEO, Richard Rosenberg, recipient of more than $18 million in compensation over the previous five years, followed that stunning report with an even more surprising announcement: 8,000 of the bank's white-collar employees would be reduced to part-time status of just nineteen hours per week—a move that made those employees just one hour shy of eligibility for benefits and saving the bank an additional $760 million while leaving thousands with a severely reduced paycheck, no health care, no paid vacation time, and no retirement.

Giannini decried the move publicly. She lamented to the press that gone were the days when "executives took a pay cut so that the lower ranks could keep their jobs." In the depths of the 1930s depression, her grandfather had ordered executives to take a 20 percent rollback in salary to keep the bank solvent—a far cry from the bank's action in its most profitable year.

Most of the time, corporate narcissism parades as the white knight galloping onto the scene to save the company from certain ruin. Self-interest may be the motive, but it isn't socially acceptable, so there must be a story—a cover—for raiding the store. In 1989 the *New York Times Magazine* published just such a story: an article written by Carl Icahn giving his rationale for draining TWA of its assets. In the article, Icahn refers to "incompetent management" as the "disease that is destroying American productivity" and justifies the actions of corporate takeover specialists like himself as the salvation of American business by destroying "the corporate welfare state." By 1992 Icahn had "saved" TWA by selling off its prized New York-to-London and Chicago-to-London routes; never buying one new aircraft, making TWA's the oldest fleet in the country; and landing the company squarely in bankruptcy court with $2.5 billion in debt. As part of the bankruptcy deal, Icahn was ousted as the chief executive and ordered to restore millions to the TWA pension fund he had raided. By 1994, the company had emerged from bank-ruptcy with limited cash and a remaining debt of $190 million that threatened to force the company out of business for good. The creditor? Who else but Carl Icahn.

From Healthy Individualism to Destructive Narcissism

Basic narcissistic needs are really healthy. These building blocks of individuality have worked quite well for American society for most of its history. Americans have long cherished the idea that individuals have a right to advance their standing in life and pursue happiness and prosperity. These healthy, narcissistic needs brought settlers to this country, created a bill of individual rights, founded the free market, developed a capitalistic econ-omy, settled the West, and pushed this country to be the wealthi-est and most powerful nation in recorded history.

But now, in parts of our society, the volume on narcissism has been turned up—way up. The pounding beat of me-and-mine has become not just a motivator but the only motivator. No longer are other considerations given equal weight with self-interest. The one and only thing that matters is that I get what I want. I will charm you, thrill you, mesmerize you, and do what-ever else is necessary to get my way.

This kind of extreme and unbalanced narcissism has wormed its way into the corporate boardroom and manifests itself in one index: quarterly reports of profit. That one figure has become the only value that is allowed to guide corporate maneuvers. Not a few companies have sacrificed long-term strat-egy and organizational health for the lure of pumping up quar-terly profits, because, in the end, short-term profit is all that really matters.

To suggest that human welfare is an important consider-ation is to be cast in the category of "sentimentally demented," as *Washington Post* columnist Richard Cohen noted. There is strong resistance to the suggestion that profit *and* the good of the workers should be considered equally in a layoff. Any action that doesn't immediately raise the bottom line is seen as irrelevant and outside the domain of business responsibility.

America's Latest Export: Layoffs

America's strongest export has always been its culture. Whether through the moving pictures from Hollywood or the academic journals from Harvard or Stanford, the American way has a strong influence on the rest of the world, especially in business, where European and Japanese business leaders in particular eye our methods to learn from our experience. American business evangelists—foreign-born, American-educated managers employed by U.S. corporations operating abroad—take the message to every corner of the globe. Whether we or the rest of the world likes it, American business practices have a strong influence around the globe.

Until recently, layoffs were primarily an American phenomenon. And to some extent, they still are, but the popularity of sacking workers for profit is growing as business owners in other countries follow America's lead. Japan is one of them. Although Japan has had a lifetime employment policy in most of its large corporations for the better part of this century, this policy is not weathering four years of deep recession. Among the Japanese companies resorting to layoffs as a means to boost earnings are Pioneer (audio/electronics), Oki Electric (telecommunications equipment), JVC (consumer electronics), and Minolta (cameras). When earnings dropped at Nissan, the influence of American management practices was clear when Nissan Tokyo promised not to resort to layoffs and Nissan USA announced on the same day a 5 percent reduction in the workforce. When Nissan Japan was questioned why the American workers were not extended the same protection as Japanese, its management replied, "It's an American company run by American people. Perhaps they could have depended more on attrition, but they chose layoffs. We asked them to meet the bottom line. The rest was their responsibility." The Tokyo-based parent company watched with interest the results at its U.S. counterpart and three months later announced layoffs in Japan.

Despite the fact that the vast majority of Japanese companies have held to the lifetime employment contract, there is a
growing trend, primarily among U.S.-educated managers, to
abandon those cultural restrictions in favor of employment at
will. The Ministry of International Trade and Industry (MITI)
has convened a committee of senior executives to study more
socially acceptable ways to "break the atmosphere" of lifetime
employment. Jiro Ushio, CEO of a halogen lamp manufacturing
company and chairman of the MITI committee, says of layoffs,
"Enlightened people are studying quietly." Aware of the enormous social obstacles he must tackle, he notes that they will have
to persuade older people, the traditional guardians of Japanese
culture, and the masses that layoffs are a better way for Japan.
      Ushio's goal of social change will be all the more difficult
now that there are strong indicators of Japan's economic recovery without having massive layoffs. In fact, there are many
economists, including Columbia Business School's Frank Lich-
tenberg, who believe that the reason Japan's economy is, on the
whole, more stable than the U.S. economy is precisely that the
Japanese have avoided wide-scale layoffs. Still, the "enlightened" push toward American-style layoffs continues.
      Even China, which has aggressively resisted any American
influence, has adopted the practice of layoffs. In 1995, the Chinese government will lay off some 2 million government workers, and further cuts are expected among the 1.3 million
government-subsidized institutions that employ 26 million Chinese citizens.
      Europe is flirting with the same ideas. Unlike Japan, most
of Europe suffers from high unemployment (Spain's rate ex-
ceeds 15 percent) and a less than adequate industrial base. With
most of Europe's workers adhering to modified socialist work
ideals, layoffs are extremely unpopular. Corporations digging to
cut costs are finding that despite the unpopularity, layoffs are
one way to lower fixed costs temporarily and increase earnings.
U.S. companies operating in Europe are beginning a trend that
is now spreading throughout the European Community. Companies like Dow Chemical are moving into the former Eastern
bloc countries, buying factories and laying off workers by the
thousands. It has created enormous resentment and a feeling

that Westerners have moved in to exploit the struggling Eastern countries. Astrid Molder, a public relations employee in the former East Germany, summed up the growing tension when she said of the old days under communism, "At least we all had jobs."

The "Enablers": Media, Consultants, and Financial Analysts

If it is true that a layoff is an ineffective management tool, why does the trend continue? How is it that corporate narcissism continues to seduce? The answer is that several key "enablers" to the culture of narcissism keep it thriving in corporate America. Through their efforts, narcissistic management tactics have taken root and become acceptable to the public.

The primary enablers of the culture of narcissism are the business media, which have done more than their share of perpetuating the myth that human welfare and social values have no place in a profit-driven business. One of the most blatant examples was printed by *Inc.* magazine in the summer of 1994 in a cover story titled "The Seven Deadly Sins of High-Minded Entrepreneurs." In this cynical article, Anne Murphy lists the business values that she considers to be detrimental to organizations. One from her condemned list of seven is, "We're just one big happy commune," referring to no-layoff policies. This kind of policy, she notes, only makes it more painful when layoffs inevitably occur. She concludes that "nice guys don't finish first" and that "virtue doesn't come cheap"—stating that environmental and social values are too costly for business to uphold. Her message is that making a profit is the only standard by which a business should be measured and run.

Most business news articles regarding corporate restructuring or layoffs either imply or state directly that these are good for the company. Polite phrases like "trimming down" or "slimming" are often used to describe what is in reality newly unemployed workers' walking to their cars, pink slips in hand. When the company performing the layoff is profitable and in no danger, words like "preemptive strike" and "preventive medicine" roll off the press. When it comes to describing the executives who are all too willing to cut jobs, the press labels them as "tough-minded" and "agents of change." In a *Business Week* article about the phenomenal layoffs at NYNEX, the CEO was described in the title as "He's Gutsy, Brilliant, and Carries an Ax." A vice president of a Fortune 500 company admits privately to reviewing and altering a feature report about his company before publication in *Fortune* ("putting the spin on the final copy" were his words). Are the business media printing corporate press releases verbatim?

Another strong enabler of narcissistic management practices are management consultants. Consultants are a diverse group, and it is common knowledge among most managers that you can hire a consultant to tell you just about anything you want to hear. A CEO who wants to hear a way to cut costs immediately can find any number of hatchet specialists for hire. In general, these consultants know two very important things about a layoff. First, it will bring relatively quick results. Because personnel costs are often an organization's greatest expense, cutting that roster can bring results fast. Second, a layoff creates another ongoing chain of problems that will keep them busy for a very long time when the company hires them to help put the pieces back together. Scratch beneath the public relations facade of almost any layoff, and you will find that the brain power behind the idea and its execution is a management consultant.

The value that most consultants provide (and they can be of tremendous value) is information and experience from other companies. Many managers may not know or have the time to find out what other companies are doing in a particular situation. Enter the consultant, with an array of experiences and information from other clients about methods that have worked and those that have not. This is an extremely valuable, albeit dangerous, role—valuable in that it provides a manager with a different viewpoint and new information on how to handle problems, dangerous for the organization in that consultants tend to be the great equalizers among organizations, perpetuating the status quo. If you are trying to do things better and cheaper than your competitor, a consultant might be of help—or he or she may lead you down the same path as your competitor.

It is in the maintenance of corporate status quo where management consultants have contributed to the spread and continuation of narcissistic management practices—take skyrocketing executives salaries, for example. Graef Crystal, a well-known compensation consultant, recently published his findings that the CEO of Home Depot was worth $39.3 million more than he was paid over the 1990–1993 years. Crystal derives his information from where most other compensation consultants get theirs: the salary survey. Based on company performance and return on investment, Crystal saw the stellar performance of Home Depot CEO Bernard Marcus as deserving of much, *much* more than he received. Yet the question must be raised: Is any human being's time for one year worth upwards of $40 million a year? CEOs are not typically primary shareholders, earning income off their investment. They are paid for their time and management skills. Bernard Marcus has done a truly magnificent job, but is his expertise worth more than $6,000 an hour? This kind of compensation advice is nothing more than the corporate version of keeping up with the Joneses. And if the Joneses happen to be milking the company to death, does that justify keeping pace with them? This is a very thin argument but essentially the one used by many consultants who advise executives on everything from compensation to customer service.

Recently a few of these professionals for hire have come around to admit that some narcissistic practices aren't always a good idea. One brave consultant, Frank A. Petro, wrote a brief editorial titled "Why Layoffs Don't Work," for the *San Francisco Chronicle* in which he condemned the practice as "a net destroyer of value." Petro is a senior vice president at CSC Index, the consulting firm where Michael Hammer and James Champy, the authors of the best-selling *Reengineering the Corporation*—a book blamed for more than a few layoffs—hung their shingle.

Petro is in the minority of consultants; the majority are still busily recommending layoffs as the panacea for whatever ails corporations. In fact, according to the *Wall Street Journal* (May 19, 1994), management consultants are finding a boom in the restructuring and layoff trend that is sweeping corporations. "This is the golden age of management consulting," said David Norton, president of Renaissance Strategy Group. As evidence, in 1994 Boston Consulting Group reported sales up 20 percent; Bain & Co., a smaller consulting firm, says 40 percent. Highly paid, very busy management consultants are making a small fortune off this culture of narcissism. Why change?

Finally, the most powerful enabler of corporate narcissism, especially from the shareholders' stake, are financial analysts. These professionals, who usually work for large financial services or brokerage firms, analyze the stock prices of a particular industry or industry segment. They watch a group of stocks for many years, becoming familiar with industry trends, company track records, and, most important, stock price trends. Their advice is heavily sought by investors, especially large institutional investors, looking to buy or sell stock. The analyst, despite having little training or day-to-day knowledge of managing an organization, interprets certain management actions as good or bad for the company's stock price based on what he or she thinks that action will accomplish. Companies that do what an analyst thinks is best will get a "buy" recommendation, investors will buy the stock, and, with any luck, the stock price will go up, increasing the value of the company.

The net result of the financial analysts' influence is that CEOs are extremely mindful of what the analysts think. When Michael Spindler, Apple Computer's CEO, took office in 1993, he announced a layoff of 2,000 employees—not to the employees or the management team but on a conference call with Wall Street financial analysts. It was no coincidence that General Mills announced it was laying off 350 workers on the same day in February 1995 that a meeting of securities analysts convened in Phoenix. Those analysts were the first to learn of the layoffs, which would be devastating to the small towns in California and Illinois where plants were to be closed.

Make no mistake about it, financial analysts have an affinity for layoffs. In fact, when Eastman Kodak announced a layoff of 10,000 workers, analyst B. Alex Henderson of Prudential Securities raised his rating of the company's stock from "hold" to "buy." Analyst Brenda Lee of Morgan Stanley hooted, "Let's sharpen that scalpel! This company built up layers of fat over how many years. There's still plenty to get out."

These three enablers—the business media, management

consultants, and Wall Street analysts—are effectively keeping the tide of corporate narcissism rolling. Without malice or conscious collusion, they are effectively stoking a fire that is consuming much of corporate America. As long as they continue to justify and validate the methods of narcissism, it will continue to spread.

The culture of narcissism has thrust its roots deep into the psyche of American business. It has become the filter through which companies and their management are viewed and valued. Employees have subscribed to the scheme that senior executives and shareholders have a right to profit from the dismemberment and cannibalism of company assets. Even the illogical idea that jobs must be lost for a company to grow has gained widespread support. The culture of narcissism is rapidly changing the complexion of the workplace into something that has little respect for human dignity or welfare.

3

After the Layoff:
The Survival Syndrome

The question we must ask is, Do layoffs solve the current corporate dilemma? Do they have the intended effect of turning company performance around? A careful look at what happens to a company after a layoff reveals an organization that is reeling from the loss of personnel, the distraction of management, and the demise of employee loyalty. The real cost of a layoff starts the morning after employees are let go.

The Morning After

The morning after a layoff, the office halls are quiet and people are at their desks. Corporate life has renewed itself, as it does every workday morning.

Managers and supervisors make the rounds of their staff offices, passing out pats on the back and admonishments of "getting back to work." The contents of vacated desks are emptied into boxes and the newly unclaimed accessories are plundered like spoils among the survivors.

Underneath his charade of normalcy, anger and mistrust brew behind the relieved half-smiles of those whose jobs were saved. Knowing they must play the game for the sake of a paycheck, their emotions fester, without expression. These anxious feelings poke and jab throughout the day, erupting in an occasional outburst from the secretary whose boss was fired or the accounting clerk who loudly berates the human resources manager. It is a toxic mix that continues to swirl and boil just beneath the surface.

Of all the destructive forces of a layoff, this is the most damaging. Contrary to what you might think, it isn't the recently departed who wield the sword of destruction but those who live with the knowledge they might be next. The survivors of a layoff, simultaneously relieved and angry, hold the greatest potential for vindictive retaliation. Common sense and corporate etiquette suggest that it might be a career-limiting move to brandish their layoff-induced rage with angry words and anxious tears. Instead these acidic feelings can seep out through the darker and secretive means of corporate sabotage.

Sabotage

Internal sabotage—everything from deliberately destoying company files to theft and embezzlement—takes a dramatic rise after a layoff. Over the years I have heard more than a few stories of what employees have done in the name of "getting even" after a layoff. Here are two of these stories, written anonymously by the perpetrators themselves:

Computer Programmer

I work on the payroll program for a large regional bank. The system I work with was one of the worst-designed systems that I had ever seen. It was using a wasteful amount of computer time and had a very bad user interface. Despite my frequent complaints, I was never allowed to modify the system in any useful ways.

The bank kept pushing my department to make the system do more than it was capable. When the higher-ups in the bank wanted to know what was going on, the other computer division directors blamed my department. They made us look really bad, like we were incompetent.

Then one day, we walked in the office only to find out that over half the department had been laid off. No one else in the computer division had been laid off, only our department. We were furious. Here they had ridden us about doing more and then they turn around and lay off half of our already overworked department!

A friend who worked next to me and I planted a logic bomb in the system. We had all the passwords that we needed to do it just right. We entered the payroll program and wrote a new section that would begin deleting the program the next time it was run. The next morning the program failed just as we had expected. But not only did it delete itself, it created a chain effect that deleted other programs on the system. Before long, the entire system was corrupted.

On payday, nobody who worked for that bank in the state of California got paid. Granted, what we did hurt the workers, but it really ruined the bank's credibility. A couple of managers in the computer division got fired. Heads rolled, and that's all that mattered to us. We had been so careful that though they suspected us, no one could prove a thing.

Stockbroker

I worked for a major Wall Street brokerage firm for two years. Everything there was cutthroat. The minute you weren't making money for the company, you were out the door. One day after a really down period on the market, management came onto the trading floor and publicly fired many of the newest traders. We were all really pissed off.

The touch-tone phones on the trading floor were actually computer links used to do block trades. With the touch of a few buttons, millions of shares of stock could be bought or sold. Each trader had his or her own locked phone.

A couple of days after all the firings, I noticed that my boss had left the floor. I walked past his station, and just as I suspected, he had left his phone key right there in the phone. I quickly picked up the receiver and punched in some major stock sells of his client's stock. Then I ran to a Telerate screen to watch the stock price plunge.

The next day when my boss discovered what had happened, he was furious. Of course, he had no idea who had done it. The whole thing ended up costing the firm over half a million dollars, and, as a result, my boss didn't get a bonus at all that year.

Not all layoff-inspired sabotage happens at the lower levels of the organization. One corporate investigations and security firm verified these instances of high-level managers' retaliating after a layoff:

- An energy company's internal report of quarterly earnings was doctored to reflect an apparent problem and then sent to Wall Street analysts.
- A chemical company's most valuable new formula was offered by a company vice president to a competitor.
- A multinational company's departed chief financial officer spent months visiting one foreign tax official after another, offering to blow the whistle on alleged tax evasions.
- A consulting firm's former officer sent bogus letters—on a company letterhead—to clients, suppliers, bankers, and competitors that were written to reflect subtle changes in the relationships. By the time the company found out what had happened, it was nearly out of business.

Sometimes sabotage is more symbolic than costly. One employee who weathered a layoff and afterward found himself demoted into a billing clerk position engaged in a bit of humorously demented sabotage by enclosing a dead roach in each bill he mailed to the firm's clients.

Another form of internal sabotage, employee theft, costs more than just a few pens and boxes of paper clips. The total cost of employee theft is now $75 billion annually. Interestingly, that figure is up from $16 billion fifteen years ago—when the layoff trend was just beginning.

Low Morale and Overwork

Most surviving employees refrain from acting out their anger in such aggressive and juvenile means. Instead, they choose more adult ways of expressing their displeasure, pushing morale to all-time lows. Complaints of stress-related illnesses and absenteeism rise dramatically. Many work hours are lost as sympathetic employees meet behind closed doors to rehash the morbid events and share their disdain for what management has done. The workplace environment becomes a toxic cesspool of bad attitudes and blame. Much to the frustration of management, no amount of preaching the it's-a-new-day-around-here gospel or sermons about discarding the past can stem the overwhelming flow of this negativity. A layoff cuts deep into the soul of the organization, and the festering wound incapacitates the corporate environment.

Beyond just bad feelings, the surviving workers are hit with a double-whammy: They must pick up the workload of the employees who were let go. All workers are pushed to work harder and longer to make up for the lost productivity. Forty-hour weeks commonly stretch to 60 and then 80 hours as a result of two jobs' being condensed into one.

George Burns, sales manager of Gamma, Chicago's largest commercial photo lab, noted after the lab laid off twenty-five employees, "Everyone has to do everyone else's job in addition to their own. I sell, supervise, and jump into the lab whenever that gets busy." His workdays lengthened from 8 or 9 hours to 12 to 14, and "you feel it," he admitted.

Nationally, layoffs have created the all-time longest workweek since the 1930s. The average workweek is now at 42 hours and includes 4.6 hours of overtime. The Big Three automakers have pushed this trend to an extreme: Their workers rack up an average of 10 hours of overtime a week and are required to labor an average of six 8-hour Saturdays a year.

Accelerating the demand for overwork is the exit of much of the company's best talent. Despite the efforts of downsizing experts to retain and protect critical talent, valuable employees often make a run for the door after a layoff. They see a layoff as a sign of instability and as threatening future layoffs, and this worry pushes them on to greener and more secure pastures.

To help patch the overwork problem, many companies have turned to temporary and contract workers to fill in where needed. Layoffs have created a booming industry for companies that broker temporary help and have pushed Manpower, Inc. past General Motors as the largest U.S. employer. Of the new jobs created in 1993, an amazing 16 percent were for temporary workers, making contingent employment one-third of the American workforce. Because temps average $140 less per week than the average permanent employee, receive no benefits, and can be fired in a moment's notice without cause, they have become an increasingly attractive option for companies struggling to survive the drain of a layoff without rehiring.

No longer just limited to the mailroom, temps are being used in virtually every capacity in the working spectrum: accountants, secretaries, and supervisors, among others. When the *Chicago Tribune* expanded its suburban coverage in 1993, it signed journalists on a temporary status, paying them far less than it pays permanent reporters. In some cases, companies are even hiring "temporary" executives to fill positions that are slated to disappear in the near future.

Effect on Company Strategies, Goals, and Projects

The aftermath of a layoff is so destructive to productivity that it makes one wonder why companies choose this path in the first place. To put the dilemma of a company that has just had a layoff in perspective, imagine that you are working on a jigsaw puzzle with thousands of pieces; then without warning, several hundred of the puzzle pieces are taken from you. You must now manipulate the remaining pieces to fit together in a way that makes sense. You spend time putting all the pieces together that fit, then figuring out which pieces must be reshaped or moved. Then you put it all together again, only to discover that new holes have cropped up, and you must reshape and move more pieces. This process goes on until you successively approximate the original picture. This is what happens in the wake of a layoff: Everyone's time and energy shift from doing the work to figuring out how the work will get done. Quality control, customer service, and productivity grind to a halt as the organization reconfigures itself.

Some processes may be permanently damaged by a layoff. A 1994 Conference Board study reported that only half of all companies made progress toward their goal of improving quality after a layoff, and only 60 percent reported seeing adequate attention to quality from employees. As for customer involvement, a cornerstone of any total quality program, less than a third reported any increase.

One of America's shining trophies of the total quality movement is Xerox Corporation. A company that once seemed invincible, Xerox had a virtual monopoly on the document reproduction market during the late sixties and seventies. But success made it sluggish, and Xerox failed to improve its processes, products, or service. Soon it found its market share was slowly being eaten by foreign competitors, which offered better and cheaper products. To turn this situation around, Xerox embarked on a massive total quality improvement campaign during the late 1980s, with every internal process the target of improvements.

Xerox did a remarkable job in improving quality and won the coveted Malcolm Baldrige National Quality Award in 1989. Because of this tremendous success, processes became streamlined and service improved, eliminating the need for many jobs. Xerox elected not to place these employees in new areas of business but to lay off 10,000 employees in 1994.

Several industry watchers wonder if Xerox can maintain the quality initiative. How can the company keep employees energized about quality if they worry about improving themselves right out of a job? C. K. Prahalad, a professor at the University of Michigan Business School who specializes in strategic management of large corporations, says, "I'm reminded of the pyramid builders, who were in no hurry to finish the pyramids because then they would be beheaded." Concerning the future at Xerox, Prahalad says, "The company cannot expect people to volunteer their commitment if they'll get punished for it."

Another unanticipated problem of layoffs is the termination of abandoned projects. Projects that were spearheaded by those who are laid off fall lifeless. One large West Coast high-tech company laid off a sizable portion of its human resources staff, many of them heavily involved in the redesign of the company's worldwide human resources computer system—a project estimated to cost the company more than $5 million, half of it already spent. The layoff and exit of several team members left the company unequipped to pick up the scattered pieces that remained, forcing it to hire expensive consultants to take over the task. The last I heard, the project had now passed the $12 million mark, with no system in place.

The cost of abandoned projects is hidden yet quite significant. Although it is true that remaining employees can step in and take over, the amount of rework and catch-up is staggering. In any significant layoff at a Fortune 500 firm, many millions of dollars are lost when work-in-progress is left dangling as pivotal knowledge is ushered out the door. As a result, money spent on the project to date is sacrificed without anything to show for the expense.

Customer service is also vulnerable to the drain of a layoff. One of the most terrifying examples of the drop in customer service after a layoff comes from the U.S. hospital industry. Carol Flynn, a registered nurse, presented a report before the prestigious National Academy of Sciences documenting fewer nurses at the bedside as a result of increased paperwork and diminished staffing levels. In a 1992 national survey of 10,000 nurses, 69 percent said the hospitals and nursing homes where they worked were chronically understaffed, placing quality of patient care at risk and triggering stress-related illnesses in the nurses themselves. Most alarming of all is the finding of a 1994 study by the Boston College School of Nursing of nearly 1,800 registered nurses in which the nurses attributed fifteen patient deaths to inadequate nurse staffing. A similar study from 1989 that reported adequate staffing levels reported no such causalities.

Hospital restructuring and the layoffs of registered nurses are jeopardizing patient care across the country, according to the American Nurses Association. Virginia Trotter Betts, president of the 205,000-member association, suggested that "someone who's pulling a slushy out of a [convenience store] machine one day . . . the next day is flushing out your arterial line." In response, Dr. James Todd, executive director of the American Medical Association, blamed the nurses themselves for the layoffs: They had overeducated themselves, he charged, and were now *overqualified* for their jobs. "They've continually pushed themselves to managerial levels," he said, "and now they're paying the price for it." Whatever the rationalization, it is clear that layoffs are jeopardizing the ability of some hospitals to serve their patients quickly and safely. The problem is severe enough to prompt Congress to fund a study of nursing layoffs by the federally funded Institute of Medicine.

For these reasons and more, the wake of a layoff is crippling to most companies. None, however, is hit as hard as the company that espouses socially responsible values and worker protection. When these companies abandon their social commitments and succumb to the quick fix of a layoff, trouble brews with previously unknown fury.

Case in Point: Hanna Andersson

Hanna Andersson, the company Gun and Tom Denhart founded in the early eighties, was at one time the largest marketer of children's apparel in the United States. The mail-order company, named for Gun Denhart's Swedish grandmother, sells handsome, high-priced Swedish children's clothes and some for adults too. It was an award-winning workplace revered for its family-leave practices, child care, participatory management, flextime, and even its lunchtime (a company-subsidized light gourmet feast in the company cafeteria). It paid part-timers and seasonal workers working 30-hour workweeks full benefits and even paid for every employee's parking. There were great salaries, cash bonuses, profit sharing, tuition reimbursement, and hefty discounts on company products. As the Denharts liked to say, "Hanna cared."

The company enjoyed many consecutive years of double-digit growth. With the company's strong knack for design and customer service, the clothes practically sold themselves to the affluent parents who were their customer base. Much, if not all, of this success rode on the design of the simple, swatch-glued catalog that showed happy, cute babies romping about in Hanna clothing. When Tom Denhart, designer of the catalog, left the business in something of a midlife crisis, things started to go downhill. A new designer, attempting to fix what wasn't broken, changed the look of the catalog, and orders plummeted. This business depended completely on a single catalog, so sales would lag for months until the next catalog was released. As a result, sales for that year inched a mere 8 percent above the previous year's, and profits slipped below 5 percent. Hanna's good nature now soured as times got tough. Hanna abandoned her lofty values, panicked, and started laying off part of the "family."

The layoff rocked the counterculture of this little company nestled in a converted Portland, Oregon, bicycle factory. Employees sat in disbelief as supervisors wept and told them that they would no longer be part of the company. The layoff decision had been made at the highest level of the company. The company president, Mary Roberts, said, "We cut quickly. We cut deeply. We did it without warning." The move was made so quickly that everyone, victims and survivors, felt betrayed.

Many at the company were dismayed that senior management had retreated from their professed ideals. After all, the company had remained profitable and sales did rebound as expected once the format of the catalog was corrected. Gun Denhart rationalizes the layoff by saying, "The right thing to do changes over time."

A year and a half since the layoff, many employees have been called back to work, but the memory of the layoff still resonates through the halls daily. Daphne Clement, one of the reemployed layoff victims, says, "We're not this family business with cushy benefits and high ideals anymore. At least not just that. It's a different atmosphere." Roberts sums up the changes noting, "There's a level of trust we might never regain."

Managers at Hanna Andersson have learned to turn a deaf ear to all the complaining about paradise lost. As Roberts puts it, "We have to get used to hearing the noise."

The downward spiral of morale at Hanna Andersson shows how much more damaging a layoff can be when it dashes the high expectations of employees. The loss of faith and trust amplifies the pain of the cuts and makes recovery all the more difficult, prompting some business writers to suggest that it would have been better if companies like Hanna Andersson had never espoused pro-employee values in the first place. As they see it, when the layoff ax does eventually swing (in their minds this is a given), the severance is all the more painful.

Are Worker Expectations the Problem?

Twisted as this advice may seem, some companies have taken it to heart. The high expectations of the workforce are the problem,

they say, not layoffs. Employees like those at Hanna Andersson
have grown to expect too much from their employers. In their
minds, employers should not be parental entities that dole out
financial and employment security. This kind of generosity only
breeds a stronger and very expensive sense of entitlement
among the workers. Instead, workers should grow accustomed
to the idea of layoffs.

This theory of "layoff inoculation" has led some senior
managers down the path of guilt-free layoffs. Since it holds that
business is helpless to avoid layoffs, the responsible thing to do
is to help the workforce accept this morbid fact. By conducting
small, successive layoffs, the company can slowly adjust worker
expectations and diminish the damaging side effects of a large-
scale layoff. Employees grow used to the fact that nobody's job
is secure and become somewhat callused to the constant trickle
of employees losing their jobs.

This was how Joann Lublin of *The Wall Street Journal* chose
to interpret the most recent downsizing survey by the American
Management Association ("AMA Survey on Downsizing," September 27, 1994). One finding of the survey was that companies
that downsized at least twice between 1989 and 1994 were more
likely to report increases in profit and productivity. Lublin's
conclusion was that repeated, smaller layoffs are good for business. As she puts it, "Reducing staff works best when the practice becomes a habit."

A deeper examination of that AMA study suggests that
Lublin's conclusions were too hasty. First, the survey was conducted by self-reports from human resources executives—the
people who orchestrate most layoffs. There is more than a little
reason for believing these executives are motivated to report
findings that support their own actions. Second, the study was a
cross section of companies, not a longitudinal study that followed each company's performance over time. Longitudinal
studies, like the one conducted by Kenneth De Meuse, professor
of management at the University of Wisconsin, almost always
find cyclical, deteriorating performance after a brief upswing in
company performance following the layoff. The findings of the
AMA survey could indicate that some companies rely on repeated layoffs to increase profits temporarily.

Most middle managers know from experience that this steady-stream method of layoffs doesn't work. It may lessen the shock of layoffs by making them a common occurrence, but many of the negative side effects still remain. These managers must shift much of their time and attention away from the real business issues to protecting their turf from more cuts and, when they aren't successful, to the difficult and stressful task of firing employees.

Burned-Out Bosses

Middle management has the hardest job of all during a layoff. This group is slammed on both sides: They have to toe the company line while laying off their staff members and worrying about the permanence of their own jobs. These managers are rarely involved in the decision to do a layoff, yet the lion's share of the responsibility for carrying it out falls on their already overburdened shoulders.

Managers are trained in business school to build a business, not tear it down, yet this is exactly what managers in today's business environment spend much of their time doing. The toll on them can be tremendous, as a rapidly rising communications executive found out. When asked to orchestrate the firing of several thousand employees several years ago, it worried him greatly, but he kept his head low and trudged forward. Last year he was promoted and a month later was asked to eliminate several thousand more positions. Within days, he began losing his appetite, had difficulty sleeping, and found himself paralyzed by the simplest of problems. He started to cry spontaneously and one day couldn't get out of bed.

The depth of this manager's personal crisis is indicative of the enormous stress layoffs have placed on otherwise competent and capable middle managers. After having laid off several hundred employees, one senior manager said, "I wondered, 'How many miscarriages is this causing? How many divorces, how many suicides?' I worked harder so that I wouldn't have to think about it."

Adam Zak, a recruiter from Chicago, tells of placing a particularly powerful executive in a job that turned out to require the firing of several hundred employees. After three months on the job, Zak said, "He was smoking, had lost weight, had trouble looking me in the eye, was extremely nervous. It seemed to me that a few months of telling people they were out the door had gone a long way in destroying his personality."

Managing the Survivors

As if all this firing business wasn't enough, middle managers are handed an even more tedious task: managing the survivors. If the number of books and training programs on the market are any indication, this is without a doubt the job surviving managers are least prepared to handle. Companies are spending millions of dollars each year on outplacement specialists and psychologists who help managers handle the emotional tidal wave that washes over the company after a layoff. These professionals provide advice on how to get staff back to business as quickly and painlessly as possible.

Managing survivors is no easy task. It takes patience and lots of time—time that otherwise would have been used to manage the business. Here are just a few of the standard recommendations given to managers about handling their surviving staff members:

▪ *Stay in control.* The novice manager often wilts in front of staff during that first postlayoff meeting as he explains that he had nothing to do with initiating the layoff and was only carrying out orders from the higher-ups. This, according to almost every expert, is the absolutely wrong thing to do. It is the equivalent of giving away power. It makes the manager look helpless and weak, fueling the already loaded blame machine. Instead the manager should appear calm and completely in control of all the circumstances. This attitude helps to rebuild an atmosphere of security and calms the fears of the staff.

▪ *Be very clear about work priorities.* The manager must sit down with each remaining employee and confirm that person's work objectives. Because of the reigning confusion created by scrambling the workload, each employee must be given clear and definitive marching orders.

▪ *Push remaining employees hard.* Part of the work-harder-so-you-won't-think-about-it school of advice, this pearl of wisdom is aimed at reducing all of the office chatter that escalates the bad feelings. If employees are too busy doing their jobs, they won't have time to worry about losing them. Work also helps build a sense of job security. "After all," thinks the survivor, if my job is so important and necessary that I have to work this hard, it isn't likely that I will also be laid off." One of the most popular managing-survivors booklets calls this "riding the herd" and "raising the bar."

▪ *Play managerial therapist.* In this role, the manager encourages employees to spill their thoughts in one-on-one sessions between the staff member and manager. These superficially confidential meetings accomplish two objectives: The manager can discover the employee's psychological barriers to getting back to work and try to remove them, and he or she can discover where (or who) the trouble spots are.

▪ *Pass out warm fuzzies.* Managers should go to their top performers and reward them with compliments and awards. As the theory goes, employees who feel needed and special are less likely to jump ship.

The demands on middle management during a layoff are enormous: They face firing those whom they have hired, must push aside their personal anxieties about their own jobs, manage an angry and demoralized staff, and reconfigure and redistribute all of the work processes. It is an enormous job that takes many long hours and not a few sleepless nights.

Resuscitating the organization after the hit-and-run impact of a layoff takes lots of time, effort, and money. The perpetrators of layoffs have raised predictions of payroll savings to a pseudoscience, but they rarely account for the hidden costs of survival. Survey after survey confirms that these managers are almost always disappointed because they didn't achieve the savings they anticipated. So they do it again and this time hope to get it right.

In the meantime, the organization is reeling. Just when it

seems to be back on its feet again, another blow strikes, knocking it to its knees. Through the trauma-induced stupor, employees can hear the ranting of senior managers demanding they do more with less and less. "You'll get used to it," they say as they push the already overworked employees back to their labor. And, indeed, as history has shown, the resilient workforce will eventually adjust. They will grow used to moving from company to company, always trying, as is human nature, to find a place where they can put down roots and contribute to something larger than themselves.

The unanswered question in all of this remains: How much more productive could the company be if so much effort weren't diverted to managing the layoff and its consequences? What if that energy was focused instead on increasing productivity and beating the competition? The answers to these questions won't come until American business terminates its affair with the seductive layoff siren.

4

We All Lose

You may be thinking, "My job is secure. My company is doing just fine. My boss and I get along great; he'd never lay me off. I'm a really hard worker, and I've had lots of successes. Layoffs don't affect me."

Think again. Even if your job is layoff proof (and few truly are), you and everyone else who continues working in the community are affected negatively by a layoff. You pay the increasing taxes that support the growing welfare roles of the first-time unemployed. Your children's education suffers as the victims of layoffs move their families to other cities and towns, leaving your school district with fewer students and greatly reduced federal and state matching funds. Your church or synagogue struggles to keep the doors open and the clergy employed as the faithful followers become hesitant to give out of reduced paychecks. You and your family suffer as teachers, police, firefighters, and road maintenance crews are laid off due to reduced individual and corporate tax bases. Make no mistake about it: Everyone in the community pays for a layoff. Look at what happened to the quiet, midwestern town of Bartlesville, Oklahoma, when the town's largest employer laid off a large portion of the poulation.

Bartlesville Blues

As you drive north from Tulsa on Highway 75, the gently rolling hills around the Arkansas River give way to the flatness of the northern Oklahoma plains. When you top the hill just past the Citgo gas station and right before you cross the Caney River, you get your first glimpse of the town that Frank Phillips put on the map: Bartlesville, Oklahoma. The skyline is a testimony to the phenomenal success of Frank Phillips: three high-rise build-ings visible from the road, all part of the Phillips legacy, to house his company, Phillips Petroleum, and the other is the hospital built to memorialize his wife of fifty years. The residents of Bar-tlesville are proud of and very grateful for the legacy this tough-minded, hardworking oilman left to them. They even named the main street of their town after him.

Bartlesville residents, like many other Americans, believe in hard work, family, and community. It is a Norman Rockwell sort of town, quirks and all. The messages tacked beneath the town's welcome sign tell you all you need to know: SQUARE DANCERS WELCOME and BARTLESVILLE IS A GARDEN CLUB KIND OF TOWN. For many of the people who move there, Phillips is a good place to make a decent living, and Bartlesville is the right place to raise a family.

Bartlesville grew as Phillips Petroleum moved from a dust bowl, wildcat drilling company in the 1930s to a major energy empire in the 1950s. The town and the company are virtually inseparable, with one in five residents a Phillips employee. Whether it is the new library, the distinctive Frank Lloyd Wright–designed community center, the restored train station where the chamber of commerce resides, or the town's only for-mal hotel, the name and generosity of Phillips are everywhere. In Bartlesville, the locals like to say, "Money in this town begins with a *P*."

Then the shocker came in 1985: Phillips quite unexpectedly announced a series of workforce reductions. This had never hap-pened in the prosperous plains town where traditionally em-ployees retired from this first and only employer. The shock of the loss pushed the town into civic denial. After so many years of seemingly unlimited success, how could this happen? The local paper, the *Bartlesville Enterprise-Examiner*, did its best to put a rosy-times-are-just-around-the-corner spin on the story.

Phillips also did its best to soften the blow for the home-town of its founder. Generous early-retirement deals were pro-vided for older workers, and severance packages equivalent to months, and in some cases years, of paychecks were handed out as the ill-fated workers walked the corporate plank. One Phillips manager remembers driving through the little town the evening after laying off several of his staff members and wondering if he had helped to destroy this community where he had lived for the past twenty-three years and where he planned to retire. "It was the worst thing we have ever done. I wonder what Frank [Phillips] would say about it if he were alive today."

The circumstances that created the layoff contributed to the denial. After all, Phillips had been a smartly managed company with a total debt-to-equity ratio of only 35 percent—extremely low compared to most other companies at the time. That's when the fortune-hungry corporate raiders, T. Boone Pickens, Jr., and Carl Icahn, set their sights on Phillips's bulging cash reserves, eagerly vying for control of the cash-rich company. Phillips managers acted to protect the company by repurchasing 50 percent of its stock at a greatly increased rate of $62 per share for a total of $4.77 billion, which pleased the shareholders by earning them a $2.15 billion profit in three months.

But what was good for those investors was devastating for Phillips, which now had a debt-to-equity ratio of 86 percent. The high debt concerned many Phillips top managers and forced them to create a plan to cut back and pay it down: They would sell off $2 billion in assets, restrict capital outlays, and part ways with some 2,500 employees, 1,000 of them in Bartlesville. Within two years, they would be forced to lay off a total of more than 5,000 employees, 2,000 of them Bartlesville residents.

The effect of the layoff on the town proved to be more devastating than any of the townspeople had expected. The real estate market collapsed. Appraisers say single-family homes declined 40 percent in value between 1984 and 1986. During the same time, commercial business permits went from eighty-nine to just seventeen per year. The city figures that $10,000 per year in retail sales were lost for every employee laid off, forcing many of the town's smaller retailers to close shop. In a chain reaction, the loss of sales tax forced the city to cut back and implement a hiring freeze. Of all the changes, the most visible and enduring came when the newly planned Plaza Office Building was reduced from thirty-nine floors to fifteen due to the reduced need for office space.

Worse yet, a dramatic fall in the price of oil spurred layoffs at other local oil companies. Many of the small, previously lucrative companies that supplied the oil fields with equipment and drilling rigs began to fight for their very existence. One company, Price Drilling, whose award-winning, Frank Lloyd Wright–designed office is a relic of better times, began dramatically rolling back its operations, spawning the same action at other supply companies.

The layoffs fueled a panic in town. "We lost a number of contracts," remembers Ernestine McAnaw, co-owner of McAnaw and Wright, one of the city's biggest real estate firms. "People were afraid there would be a takeover, that they would be out of a job. They walked away from their contracts and defaulted on their deposits." Others pulled their savings from banks, paying hefty penalties for early withdrawal in an effort to beat a bank failure they feared was just around the corner. Even the school district reacted, contemplating layoffs in an effort to prepare for the worst.

Almost ten years later, life in Bartlesville has returned to normal. Phillips is profitable and hiring. The memory of friends and neighbors who are now living in other cities is slowly being replaced by new faces drawn to jobs in Bartlesville. Yet the effects of the layoffs remain. As one Phillips employee said: "The memory of those layoffs never goes away. Every time I buy a car or take a vacation, I first look to see how the company is doing. If there is even one smidgen of a chance that things aren't good, I won't spend the money."

Bartlesville is a microcosm of what happens in every community during a layoff, even towns and cities that are economically more diverse than Bartlesville. In communities of all sizes, the values of community and family are cherished above those of work, yet it is the work that allows community to thrive. When the work diminishes, the bonds of community are stretched to the limits and sometimes break. Communities like Bartlesville do survive the onslaught of a layoff, but they often pay a price for years, even decades, afterward.

The Power of Threat

Communities of all sizes tremble at the hint of a layoff. Knowing what that economic domino effect can do to a local economy, government officials are pressured to try to avert a layoff.

Tax Breaks

Shreveport, Louisiana, the onetime international center of the oil industry, is a sleepy southern town that draws heavily on a residual oil field supply trade for economic stability. In the recession of the early 1980s when oil prices fell, Shreveport's economy was thrown into the depths of what the rest of the country called a recession but looked to the locals more like a depression. Businesses were boarded up, banks failed, and many lost their jobs as small and midsize businesses faltered under the strain. Except for two large manufacturing plants, a General Motors truck facility, and an AT&T communications equipment plant, paychecks were hard to find.

Then AT&T, citing "market deterioration," laid off 6,600 in Shreveport. AT&T corporate headquarters in Baskins Ridge, New Jersey, had ordered the layoffs in an attempt to manage its worldwide business, but many Shreveport residents resented that AT&T had chosen such a poor time to dump workers at the local plant. It only made a bad situation much worse for the Shreveport community.

Almost ten years later, in 1993, the management of the AT&T plant asked local governments to rescind a tax on $55 million in product inventory, which would amount to a tax break of more than $1 million. If the breaks were not granted, AT&T hinted, it might close the local distribution center and lay off 112 employees. But if it was granted the breaks, it promised to add twelve to fourteen new jobs at the distribution center.

Local officials, living in one of the poorest states in the United States, were caught between the fear of losing jobs or losing tax dollars. Both were needed desperately; neither could be sacrificed.

At the first Caddo Parish Commission meeting after AT&T made the request, the company was blasted for asking for tax breaks when only two months earlier it had laid off ninety-six workers. Commissioner Hersey Wilson asked, "How can we give you millions of dollars in taxpayer money and you can't give us assurances that our citizens who have spent the better part of their lives working at AT&T will have a place to work?"

Despite the protests and resentments, some of the government agencies affected reluctantly granted the tax breaks. It was simply a matter of choosing between the lesser of two evils. What would be worse: citizens' losing their livelihoods or taxpayers' picking up the slack left by granting the company tax breaks? In this tightly knit, family-oriented community, the choice was made to protect the jobs of friends and family. Somehow they would find a way to make up the lost tax revenue.

Southeast of Shreveport are the small towns of Hodge and Jonesboro, Louisiana. In a similar turn of events, a large paper bag manufacturer, Stone Container, threatened to devastate the bayou country of Louisiana's Jackson Parish by closing a plant located there. All players moved quickly to prevent the closure. The state legislature voted Stone a $3 million tax break (this in a state that has had repeated budget deficits in the millions of dollars over the past fifteen years). The two towns granted the company abatement from local taxes (Stone being the largest corporate taxpayer in both towns). The local labor union coughed up a 7 percent pay reduction over two years. Even the towns' merchants agreed to give a 10 percent discount to Stone employees—both those who would be laid off and those who would continue working at reduced wages. Despite all these concessions, Stone couldn't guarantee the plant would remain open for more than a year.

Real Estate Breaks

Companies that threaten layoffs are also winning favorable real estate breaks. Owners of large warehouses and office buildings where many large companies rent office and storage space are more than willing to negotiate lowered rents in the face of losing a primary tenant all together. Since the mid-1970s it has been a common practice for companies to build office and warehouse buildings tailored to their specific needs, occupy the building, and then sell it with an agreement to lease the space back from the new landlord. So when the company threatens to cut back on space, the landlord is faced with trying to rent a building that will need modification to fit a new tenant—if one can be found that needs such large square footage. Finding new tenants can mean having the building empty for several years, and the loss of rent can mount into the millions.

Eased Environmental Regulations

Consider what happened in 1982 when the U.S. automakers, blustering about threatened layoffs to the press, went to the White House to seek a repeal of certain environmental regulations on new automobiles. In the name of saving jobs, the Reagan administration obliged and significantly rolled back environmental requirements. The communities of Los Angeles, New York, Washington, D.C., and other cities that suffer from high automobile pollution have paid dearly for those jobs.

Credit Breaks

The threat of downsizing is especially difficult for small businesses that supply the downsizing companies. Small business profit margins are often quite narrow and have little buffer. When the primary customers of these businesses delay payment or, worse, threaten to stop purchases altogether by shutting down a local site, small business is caught in a bind. Does it extend more credit in the hopes of not losing a customer, or terminate the relationship and risk bankruptcy? Its's not a pretty choice either way.

The Rebound of Joliet—and the Price It Pays

If any region of the United States is a testimony to the downward spiral of communities after successive layoffs, it is the Rust Belt. Towns struggling to survive after massive corporate cutbacks watched their community infrastructure disintegrate before their eyes. Roads and public buildings suffered from disrepair. Hospitals and schools delayed or abandoned plans for long-needed additions and remodeling. Most difficult of all was the job of attracting new business to replace the tax base lost when the others laid off or closed down.

In 1984, one of these Rust Belt towns, Joliet, Illinois, experienced a major layoff and racked up the highest unemployment rate of any other town or city in the country: 27.6 percent. Ten years later, the town was still struggling to generate new jobs.

That's when the citizens decided to welcome legalized gambling.

The town of Joliet, Illinois, has had several nicknames over the years. In the very early years of this century, it was known as Stone City, after the millions of tons of limestone quarried from under Mt. Joliet. When the mines shut down, it became known as Steel City, after the rolling mills and blast furnaces that once scarred the face of its landscape. And since 1858, there has been the bleakest name of all: Prison City, after the medieval-style prison built on its outskirts.

Industry may have been kind to Joliet's workers, but it was devastating to the look of the town. The poet Carl Sandburg once wrote of Joliet:

> On the one hand the steel works
> On the other hand the penitentiary
> Santa Fe trains and Alton trains
> Between smokestacks on the west
> And gray walls on the east . . .

However it is described, Joliet has always been a hardworking, blue-collar kind of town. No doubt, this reputation is what first attracted Caterpillar to build a plant there.

Since the depression of the 1930s, Caterpillar has been very good for Joliet and surrounding Will County. From its opening, Caterpillar had consistently made good profits and brought jobs to Joliet. By 1981, Caterpillar recorded its largest profit ever: $578.9 million. But in 1982, the big CAT, as it's known, started laying off workers. At first, it was only a few. Then it was a few more, but none in Joliet. But by the time 1983 rolled around, Caterpillar had laid off over half its 5,000 employees in this town of just fewer than 80,000 residents. Unemployment skyrocketed, and more than 15 percent of the population fell below the poverty line. According to Joliet's third-generation merchant Frank Turk, Jr.: "We hit the low point in Joliet's history. . . . We knew we had to do something drastic."

After a decade of struggling while it witnessed its population decline and the boarding up of its downtown, Joliet did something drastic: It approved the docking of floating casinos in the Des Plaines River that flows through the center of town. Now, with four riverboats in operation, the economic climate of Joliet is changing. The boats attract about 18,000 people a day, each on average losing $61 each. Receiving $1 for each passenger, the city of Joliet collected approximately $23 million in 1994, or nearly one-quarter of the city's annual budget. Collectively, the boats have created 3,400 jobs that pay on average $8 per hour plus tips for most workers. In addition, more than 6,000 construction jobs have been spawned due to the construction of gambling facilities and new homes for the workers.

Joliet has finally been able to catch up with the losses from the Caterpillar downsizing. The city has repaved fifteen miles of roads, replaced aging sewer pipes, eliminated the annual $25-a-car tax, lowered water bills, and put $6.8 million into neighborhood improvements, which include brick walkways and new streetlights downtown. A local resident, Wayne Barnett, has even led a grassroots movement for property tax rebates since in the wake of the layoffs, Joliet property taxes were forced upward to 3.2 times more than the national average.

The fact that Joliet's economy and tax base has shifted so quickly and heavily to gaming, as gambling proponents like to call it, has some residents worried. There are already proposals on the table to open five riverboats in nearby Chicago and additional boats in suburbs between the two cities. The result would most definitely mean a dramatic drop in attendance, and that would bring layoffs.

Others are uncomfortable about becoming dependent on gaming companies whose history has shown them to be, well, not exactly dependable or ethical. "The river boat owners are going to take $300 million out of this community and give back $18 million or $20 million. That's not how you save a community, that's how you kill it," said Reverend Lynda Hawkins. "They will stay here until they've drained this community dry; then they'll float on down the river."

For now, Joliet doesn't seem to have many other options. In the decade since the layoffs, Ruth Fitzgerald, president of the Will County Chamber of Commerce, has been successful in attracting a number of smaller businesses to the area but none with the employment power of the casinos. While the gambling dollar is admittedly fickle and the casino jobs pay far less than the old jobs at Caterpillar, Joliet officials hope for the best. After all, they rationalize, having some economic stimulus is better than nothing at all.

Government Assistance, Please

Whether it is Bartlesville, Joliet, or Anytown, USA, one fallout of a layoff is always the same: Displaced workers are forced into the financial care of the government through programs like unemployment benefits, welfare, and Medicaid.

In New England, the layoff of more than 323,000 workers between 1991 and 1993 is credited with the dramatic rise in first-time, two-parent families who are now dependent on public assistance. In the state of Vermont alone, that same period saw a 200 percent rise in the number of these families who are receiving benefits. John D. Bamford, the assistant director of economic and social services for the Rhode Island Department of Human Services, observed, "The type of growth we're seeing on a monthly basis is phenomenal and there is no lessening up."

Not only are the remaining employed taxpayers saddled with supplementing the income of the newly laid off, they must also foot the bill for their medical care. In fact, many laid-off workers are prevented from taking the low-paying, part-time jobs available because the income will be just enough to disqualify them from receiving child care assistance and Medicaid. As noted by one social services' economic services program administrator for the state of North Carolina, "By the time they pay their bills they have nothing left for medical care." The state of North Carolina recorded in 1993 a 15 percent increase in those eligible to received Medicaid benefits. Once again, the majority of this increase came from first-time-unemployed, two-parent households.

The burden on the taxpayer doesn't stop with financial assistance. The laid-off workers are no longer taxpayers, so surviving workers have to pick up the slack. No one knows more about this than the taxpayers of Washington State, where the Boeing Co. accounts directly or indirectly for nearly one out of every ten

tax dollars taken by the state. When the giant aircraft manufacturer announced layoffs in 1993, the message went straight to
the state legislature in Olympia. The 35 percent cuts at Boeing
translated into $400 million in lost taxes for the state. Within
days, proposals were on the table to raise college tuition, halt
school reform programs, and, of course, increase taxes. The state
budget director, Ann Daley, responded to the lost revenue and
program cuts by admitting "It makes it tempting to say, 'Let's
just fix this now' and leave these problems for another day."

Helping a region to come back after major layoffs can be
very expensive for the taxpayer. After the Northwest was hit
hard by layoffs from closing timber mills in 1993, the federal
government poured $75 million into the region, part of a total
$1.2 billion pledge to help create new jobs.

Retirement: For Whom?

One explosive aspect of layoffs has been planted twenty years or
so into the future. In that time period, many workers who have
bounced from one layoff to the next will not have adequate pensions to support them through retirement. The care and financial
support of these older retirees will fall on their families, the community, and the taxpayer. Since 1975, the American workforce
has grown from 65 to 93 million workers, yet during this same
period, the percentage of workers covered by pensions has gone
steadily down. Currently, less than half of all workers are covered by a pension. And the news gets worse: If downsizing is
here to stay, as so many executives have concluded, increasing
numbers of workers who would otherwise be covered by pension plans will be shuffled from job to job throughout their careers, reaching retirement with few or no benefits. With a
faltering social security system, someone will have to pay for the
support of retired-but-broke workers.

In any community there exists a cause-and-effect relationship. Anything that happens to one aspect of the community
produces an effect on the remainder of it. This has been and will
be true of layoffs. When so many in the community lose their
jobs and livelihoods, even temporarily, the rest of us feel the
impact of their loss. No one is exempt. There is no place to hide.

Part Two
The Anatomy of a Layoff

There is no way to do a painless layoff. Someone must break the trust. Someone must decide who stays and who goes. Someone must deliver the message.

The only possible way to carry out these tasks in today's litigious environment requires a good measure of secrecy and sometimes even blatant deceit. Plans must be made and held in the strictest of confidence until the moment of announcement. In the interest of minimizing the threat of sabotage, employees must be led to believe that they are employed and secure until the day of the layoff.

Managers scramble to protect their valuable staff members from the swing ax. They trade head counts and funding, doing whatever they can to protect their domain from the ravages of the cutback. The environment becomes heated with the pressure of the task and the politics of reduction.

The human resources department plays a key role in the planning and execution of a layoff. HR offices become command central for organizing and processing the reconnaissance information about employee performance and value. Normally a relatively mundane and sidelined staff function, this department often finds its highest power and visibility during a layoff.

5

A Mass Execution

The method of a mass layoff is deliberately devious and cloaked in secrecy. Planning, organizing, scheduling, controlling, deception, and craftiness are all part of the scheme. Management wants a quick cut that protects the assets of the company yet is gentle and compassionate toward those who are let go. These two objectives are, in large measure, self-canceling; to accomplish the first requires considerable compromise on the second.

Most companies cannot afford to tell workers of a layoff prior to handing out the pink slips. There is too much opportunity for sabotage and work slowdowns. The anticipation of a layoff can be extremely detrimental to production. By far, the preferable method is to keep most of the details quiet until the very day of the layoff. That way, the strike is clean: The nabbed workers leave, and the rest get back to business.

But this method of conducting a layoff, and all the manipulation involved in carrying it out, is the least favorable for the employees. With notice and time to plan, employees who know they will be losing their jobs can begin to accept the fact, rearrange their finances, and begin looking for another job *before* they are unemployed and become increasingly less marketable. They can prepare themselves for the loss and begin the transition into a new job. Nevertheless, it is the best interest of the company that prevails in this situation.

Some years ago, I was involved in orchestrating a mass layoff. Here is what happened.

A Corporate Execution

Accepting a job from a Silicon Valley personal computer maker as manager of organizational development was one of the riskiest career moves I ever made. With several graduate degrees in business and psychology and having worked with two other Fortune 100 companies, I was sufficiently armed with the tools of the trade. The risk, and it was sizable, lay in the company itself. Previously a fast-growing competitor stretching to stay ahead of a continually evolving personal computer technology and market, it was now floundering with a diverse and poorly stratified product line. The company made solid and reliable computers, but they lacked the features that both the office and home markets now demanded. As competitors responded to these demands, the company's sales started to slip. Company management was scrambling for answers.

My hiring was to be one of those answers. My job was to help in streamlining the "human" processes within the company. The breadth of my job encomposed all of the channels within the organization where ideas and information flow from one person to the next and eventually develop into products and services. For example, I might try to determine whether it was more efficient to have research and development engineers in a separate department from manufacturing engineers or would make more sense to have a cross-functional team of engineers organized around a specific product.

I was no stranger to organizational change. Every job I had held since college had been involved in some sort of organizational change. After all, most companies don't see the need to have an industrial psychologist like myself on staff until they run headfirst into the wall of human resistance to change. I have been in every step of a corporate restructuring from drawing the scenarios to implementing the structure, to helping managers handle the change, to evaluating the effectiveness of the change. A new structure may be perfect on the drawing board, but if the players don't support it, it is doomed to failure. A large part of my job was to make sure there was adequate support for the changes every step of the way.

The pressure and tension that were on the organization began to settle on my shoulders with my first day on the job. Everywhere I looked and began to dig, I found departments and business processes that had grown organically to fill needs as they appeared. This technology was needed or that microchip was now part of a new product, and, suddenly, five people were hired to form a department to handle it. What had evolved over time was an organization chart that meandered, twisted, and turned without much logic to the outside observer.

Despite the overgrown maze of departments and grab-bag job titles, company insiders saw a certain familial logic to it all. Many of the employees had been around since the early days and knew by experience how to make things happen. In fact, some highly regarded managers in the company derived much of their power and reputation from the fact that they knew who to call in any given situation. As the company had grown, however, it had become difficult for even the old-timers to understand the flow of business through the organization. Consequently, some very important items of business became lost in the maze of many hands.

More than once I doubted my own ability to do the job I had been hired for. It was tough enough to learn all the various high-tech constituents of the computer business, much less crack the code of an enigmatic organizational structure. When I added to that the fact that a strong emphasis on "partnering" had come to a mean a nonconfrontational, nonagressive organizational culture, I wondered if the company would tolerate the kind of massive change that would be necessary for success. Without that kind of change, I would never be successful in my role.

So you can understand why I was relieved when in executive staff meeting six months after my arrival, the CEO announced that the company would have to lay off at least 400 employees. With production costs continuing to rise and revenues slipping, everyone present agreed there was little other choice. The outcome of that meeting was that it would be my department's responsibility, assisted by Human Resources, to plan and implement the layoff. This might just be the event that was needed to start the momentum of change.

I felt both relief and guilt—relief for the perfect opportunity to analyze and streamline all essential company processes, guilt because I knew from experience how painful a layoff can be. This was a chance for me and my team to show how much value we could add to the company—a chance that was also regrettable because many employees would lose their jobs in the process.

The Plan

Without revealing the eventuality of layoff to anyone outside that meeting, we launched a two-month-long, thorough analysis of every organizational process, in every department throughout the company. A troop of volunteered company managers and I virtually plastered the conference room with brown paper and covered it with flow charts, diagrams, and Post-it notes. Nothing was spared or sacred as we tore apart every inch of the company looking for what was essential and nonessential, what should be internal and what could be outsourced. At the end of the two months, we presented to the executive committee our findings and wrestled agreement to our conclusions from everyone present.

The plan was then set in motion. Everything that fell into the nonessential category would be eliminated. Employees who were affected would be absorbed by other departments or laid off. With the help of senior management, we made and remade lists of employees to be laid off until everyone was certain they had cut as far as they dare go. Once the list was finalized, the planning of the layoff began.

We began the planning process by meeting with selected human resources managers every day for a month and a half prior to the day we would hand out pink slips. Meeting privately, we commandeered a secluded conference room as the coordination point for the day of the layoffs. This was command central—the place where the predestined unemployed names were bantered about and where the gory details of how their employment would be severed were devised. We had met in this room every day during lunch (this time was chosen so that it wouldn't raise any suspicions), planning every minute and scripting every word that would be said. Everything had to be confidential; nothing could be left to chance.

We had to plan for every possible contingency imaginable. If someone were to become violent, we had security guards on standby (not visible, though, for fear this might incite violence). If someone were to become upset or even disoriented, we had counselors on standby. In case someone was to become vindictive, we had privately coordinated with one authorized person in management information services to have passwords revoked at the moment each marked employee was being told of his or her jobless fate. We had even identified the nearest exit to each employee so that he or she could be whisked out of the building with the least amount of disruption. It had to be a clean, surgical strike.

Working to make a layoff happen is something of a selfless act because the primary goal is to protect the company's interests. For us this meant two things: maintain complete secrecy until the last possible moment to prevent a premature disruption of work and protect the company from possible sabotage by the newly discharged employees. Oddly enough, we were working to protect the company from its own employees.

The inside of our conference room was plastered with Post-it notes on which all the names and locations of employees were written. We planned that there would be three people—one human resources manager, the employee's supervisor, and an outplacement representative—in a predetermined conference room as we told the employee that he or she no longer had a job. Each of these meetings would last fifteen minutes, and we scheduled them every half-hour for the entire day. Using a number of teams, we would have it all completed by 4:30 that afternoon.

The language that was used in these meetings had to be absolutely clear. For legal reasons and because most people in shock don't comprehend much, we memorized the speech. It went something like this:

> We regret to inform you that due to a recent reorganization, your job no longer exists. We made every effort to find a place for your skills in the new organization but have been unable to do so. This decision is not a reflection on your job performance or skills but the result of business changes. It has been reviewed at the highest level of organization and will not be reversed.

You will be escorted to your desk and allowed to pack your personal belongings. You are to be off the premises within the period of one hour and are not to return. Should you have forgotten any personal belongings, they will be mailed to you. The company has provided an outplacement center at another location to which it is suggested that you report at 8:00 A.M. tomorrow. Your supervisor will now provide you with a packet that explains your severance pay and benefits. Included in that packet is a letter of final settlement [absolving the company from any further liability], which you must sign in order to receive your severance pay. If you choose not to sign it at this time, please be aware that this offer of severance pay expires at the end of business today.

Everything that was to happen that day was orchestrated. For two days prior to the layoff, I held confidential training sessions with company managers, teaching them exactly what to say and what not to say to the laid-off employees. More important, I admonished them to pull together the remaining employees—the "survivors," as I called them—after the layoff and begin rebuilding the "team." After all, it was in the best interests of the company that everyone put this incident behind them and move the business forward. I even suggested that one way to help employees overcome their anxiety and sense of loss was to *increase* their workload so that there was less time for gossip and angry escalations.

Planning for a layoff is kind of like playing God—you know more about what the future holds for those around you than they do. I remember standing in line at the copy machine or sitting in the cafeteria eating lunch listening to other employees chatting away about their weekend—their kids—their vacation, all the time knowing that their lives were about to come to a perilous juncture. It sometimes crossed my mind how deceived they would have felt if they had only known that the smiling face across the hall was secretly plotting their departure. I told myself that it was for their own good that they didn't know. Let them enjoy their time up until the last moment. Besides, we had the company to protect, and we all knew what havoc angry employees could create.

"Black Friday"

On the day of the layoffs we met at 5:00 A.M. for a "synchronization" meeting. All the meeting schedules and severance packages were prepared and organized for each team. There was a lot of nervous joking and laughter as we made the final preparations. We all agreed to meet after the day was over to relax over cocktails and debrief the events of the day. With that, we all dispersed into the jungle of corridors and cubicles to bring about what would from that day on be known as Black Friday.

The first task of the day was to distribute a memo to the desk of every employee who was scheduled to be laid off. Noticeably brief, the memo simply told the employee that a meeting had been scheduled at a particular time and place. This meeting was "to supersede all prior commitments" and "attendance was absolutely mandatory." Distributed before any of the unsuspecting employees arrived for what I'm sure they thought was another day of work, it would quickly become the mark of death once the word was out.

The first two layoff meetings I held went surprisingly well. The newly unemployed employees simply stared at me or the papers in front of them, signed the letter, collected their check, and went home. One even joked about having a long lunch planned for that day anyway. My cohorts and I were under a tight schedule so it was just as well they took it so well. We raced out of the corporate headquarters after the second meeting and drove to a building located across town.

On the drive over I remember thinking about my role as a psychologist, a *healer*, in all of this. Had I forsaken the healing role, or was this one of those painful losses in life out of which grows something far better? The only way I could get through the day was to remind myself that this was for the good of the company, and, if the company succeeded, we all benefited. It might be painful now, but there could be no growth without pain.

As I entered the building, I sensed a dark mood over the office. It was clear from the faces of the employees in the hallway that word had gotten out about what was happening. No one smiled or dispensed the usual greeting. They looked at me and scurried away almost as if they thought I had some power to choose my next victim. Didn't they know I was just doing my job?

I was aching inside. As I walked through those winding corridors of cubicles, I felt as if I was in a surreal world, suspended between the tug of empathy for those who were being laid off and my own commitment to the company. In my head I knew that this was a necessary pruning, but in my heart I saw myself sitting on the other side of the table—stunned at the news that the job to which I had given so much was seen as unnecessary and discarded. How lonely it must feel to no longer be part of the group. How terrifying it must be to face the imminent loss of a paycheck.

The next meeting didn't go so well. Once we were all seated, I started giving my speech to someone who was no stranger to me. Linda was a secretary I had worked closely with on several projects. I had known that things weren't working out between her and her boss, a vice president, but she had always done a great job for me. We avoided looking at each other as I spoke. When I finished, she didn't move for several long seconds; then she stood up and paced the length of the room and started wringing her hands. "What am I supposed to do?" she pleaded, not waiting for the answer that we couldn't give. "I am a single mother, my parents are gone, and I just closed on a house two weeks ago. I *need* my job," she said as the tears started to flow. My reaction was to offer some comfort, at least offer some words of encouragement, but we had been strictly warned by the company attorney not to do anything of the sort. It was for the good of the company that we restrain ourselves, lest we make some passing promise that would end up in court later. We all just sat there until she gathered her papers and walked out. From that point on, I don't remember many of the details of our day, as the rest seemed to fly by. I do remember, however, that by the time we had all gathered back over much needed drinks, I had kept my schedule. We had eliminated 400 jobs for the company.

The Executioners' Party

Our little party turned out to be something less than a pick-me-up. Richard, the vice president of human resources to whom we all reported, began the meeting by thanking all of us for our hard work and dedication. Then he did something that hadn't appeared on my strict schedule, catching me completely off guard. He began reading the names of those in Human Resources who would be laid off. These were my comrades, some of the ones with whom I had worked so closely in our daily meetings. I quickly scanned the room, searching the faces of those whose names had been called. Judging from their calm expressions, it was clear that Richard had had the decency to fill them in ahead of time.

The room was darkened by what had just happened. Except for the whispered good-byes, the brush of gentle embraces, and the intermittent sound of a muffled tear or two, there wasn't much left to say. Jill, one of the now ill-fated employees who had worked almost full-time for the past month coordinating the layoff, referred to feeling like a convicted murderer who had recently been put to death in the California gas chamber. Her comment cut us all deeply as we realized that we, after performing our duties that day, were no longer needed.

I was angered by the timing of Richard's layoff announcement. Suddenly the tables had been turned on those of us who had been turning them for everyone else all day long. Using the very same secrecy and coolness of manner we had practiced, Richard told four of our colleagues they no longer had jobs. Why didn't I know about this? I felt deceived and as if my loyalty to the company had been violated. We were the good guys, and we deserved better treatment than this.

Then it dawned on me. How was what Richard had done to us any different from what we had done to the rest of the company? We had been secretly plotting the departure of coworkers for months, and then we had suddenly sprang it on them, giving them little time to react and no opportunity to respond. They must surely be feeling the anger, helplessness, mistrust, and pain that flooded over me now. If this had been brewing behind the scenes, what else was planned that we hadn't been told about yet?

I found it hard to leave the office that night. I'm not sure why, but I remember it was somewhat comforting to put my desk back in order after this chaotic day. Not long after I began my housecleaning, Susan walked into my office and slumped into a chair. Susan was a bright, motivated human resources manager, and I always enjoyed her company. She looked straight at me and without the usual smile that accompanies corporate whining, she said, "I don't ever want to do this again. We did a perfect job today and I couldn't be less proud of it." The lump I had been pushing down all day rose in my throat, and if I answered her at all, I can't remember it.

The Lessons of Layoff and Survival

The lesson my staff and I learned that day about layoffs is the lesson of all survivors. Recently, a friend of mine, while dining in a trendy San Francisco restaurant, witnessed a woman walk in the front door, yell a few words in Chinese, and then shoot a woman sitting at a corner table. Panic ensued as the diners jumped for cover under their tables, behind doors, and wherever else they could find some shield between themselves and the armed woman. When my friend recounts this tragic scene, he tells of the many months following that incident when some small occurrence—a few words of Chinese, someone yelling, even looking up from a restaurant table to see a lone person standing in the doorway—would send him into a panic. His palms would sweat, his heart would jump, and the sound of that fatal shot would ring in his ears. This is the lesson of survival: The effects of trauma live on long after the danger has passed. So it was with those who survived the layoff.

Being a part of the layoff—standing by and witnessing it unfold—had a traumatic side effect that went far beyond the actual pain of terminating employees. The secrecy that border-lined on deceit and the surviving employees' loss of control over their own destiny attacked the very essence of their human dignity. It severely traumatized the very employees the company was depending upon to pick up the pieces.

The company reeled under the effect of that trauma for well over a year after the layoff. Many of the top performers, scared that they might be next, started defecting to competitors. Some of those who remained became bitter and disgruntled. These employees so idealized the days before the layoff, when the company was still a "family," that they privately referred to it as "Camelot." Many employees became unwilling to give the little extra effort that can often make the difference between mediocrity and real success in the marketplace.

The layoff had been well planned and executed. It was a bittersweet reward to know that because I did my job so well, many of the "survivors" were disenfranchised by the layoff. Almost every employee had been involved in writing reports and preparing figures on what he or she did for the company. Unknown to them at the time, those data were used to make decisions about who would go and who would stay. Because we had been so careful to keep the layoff confidential, it was quite a surprise to everyone outside our tight circle. Very quickly they realized that this was something that had been planned behind their backs for some time prior, and it was that fact alone that eroded their trust and loyalty to the company.

What we didn't know at the time was that we were also cutting into the soul of the organization. We were destroying that sacred place in the very center of the company where the essence of loyalty and community reside. It was as if we lined up all of the employees and ripped up the social contract between the company and employees right before their faces. We ignorantly proclaimed that loyalty and even job performance meant nothing. It would take several years of rebuilding for the company to regain the lost trust and motivation of its employees.

The final blow came almost six months to the day from that Black Friday. On that day, Marshall, the CEO, resigned. Not only was it not a surprise, it was probably long overdue. Many of us suspected that it was Marshall's mismanagement of the organization that had thrown the company into the mess it was in and caused us to have to lay off so many of our coworkers. Later that afternoon the evening paper reported Marshall's resignation and the payment of a $4 *million* golden parachute! That $4 million was roughly equal to the savings recouped from all of the layoffs for the first year. All those people had lost their jobs, had their families uprooted and their futures compromised so that one man, someone who had seemingly added little value and may have cost the company plenty, could receive "fair" compensation.

That was the day this corporate executioner decided to put his hatchet away. I learned the hard way that while the initial cut of a layoff is painful, the aftermath can be deadly.

6

One-on-One Executions

Not every layoff happens on such a large scale. In fact, every day in companies of all types and sizes, layoffs occur with no announcement, no fanfare, and no newspaper coverage. These are targeted one-on-one executions, and because they are singular and tacit, they are never counted in the layoff statistics. But make no mistake: Underneath this cloak of silence, they are very real.

Firing vs. Layoff

The kind of singular layoff of which I speak is not a firing for poor job performance. Consistent, accurate, and thorough performance evaluation is one of the most powerful tools a company has to maintain performance.

Admittedly, managing someone else's behavior is tough. Setting the limits of what other adults should and should not do is a situation ripe for conflict. Yet anyone who has managed a business, regardless of size or scope, knows that managing other employees' performance is critical to managing the business. Someone has to set the standards. Someone has to measure the progress. Someone has to give the feedback. And sometimes somebody has to get fired. It's just a fact of life.

Some jobs and some people just don't mix well. Good managers learn early in their careers the tools of motivating and coaching their employees. They also learn how to recognize a hopeless situation and how to fix it. Painful as it may be, they know that allowing a poor performer to stay onboard can be damaging beyond just the job that isn't getting done. Coworkers see what is tolerated, and standards start to slip. The consistently conscientious high producers resent pulling the dead weight along, and morale takes a dive.

The Value of Good Performance Management

Managing and evaluating employee performance is a critical task for a successful manager. It isn't difficult, but it takes time, effort, and plenty of observation. Actually, an employee's abilities and skills often speak for themselves. Coworkers know who can produce and who can't. The observant supervisor knows it too.

Thorough performance management is the hallmark of the truly great manager. This manager cares enough to track each employee's performance and offer support and coaching when it is needed. Poorly performing employees who are left on their own drag themselves and their coworkers down. For the sake of the company and the good of the employee, the successful manager won't let this happen. Poor performers are given attention and support; if they don't improve, the more drastic step of reassignment, or termination, may follow. The outcome of this kind of performance management is a workforce that is trimmed of the dead weight. Under such a thorough system, only those who are contributing to the organization survive.

In an appropriately managed organization, job performance and a layoff have nothing in common. When all employees either meet or exceed performance standards, performance becomes an ineffective criterion.

When the command is given to lay off employees, what can a manager do? As noted, selecting employees to be laid off on job performance is useless. Besides, basing a layoff on job performance is a lot of work, wrought with human resources red tape, and it risks costly litigation. The cuts could be made according to seniority, but that would sack the new, highly prized Ph.D. from Harvard who was recently lured away from a competitor. The only feasible choice for most managers facing mandatory staff cuts is to base the layoffs on essential job functions.

Layoffs and Essential Job Functions

Determining which jobs are essential to the business and which aren't sounds relatively straightforward. It begs the question: What can we live without and still run a healthy business? Despite how simple it sounds, this approach is also difficult for most managers. Often consultants are hired and detailed studies performed to analyze what is absolutely necessary for success and what can be discarded. Even with a thorough analysis, the question, "*What* can we live without?" becomes confused with, "*Whom* can we live without?" Sometimes if the right "what" is cut, it means laying off the wrong "whom." All in all, there is no easy or painless way to compose the layoff list.

Devising the list takes a lot of work and requires some hard choices. Not a few managers have looked down this path and found it to be much too cumbersome. They envision an easier way. Wouldn't it be simpler if a few staffers chose to resign? Perhaps with a little help, these expendable employees might just leave on their own. A heavy-handed nudge might push them over the employment edge. There's no severance pay, no lawsuits, no bad press, no lengthy documentation or grievance hearings. There is a party, they go away, and the reduction target is met. Perfect.

Singular Execution Techniques

Only a minority of managers use these singular layoff techniques. Most find them distasteful, uncomfortable, and somewhat unethical. But they are used often enough across all kinds of organizations and industries to have affected many thousands of workers. These victims of a layoff rarely show up in statistics or news reports. They quietly exit through the back door, often with a badly battered self-confidence in hand.

The first time I saw one of these techniques used, I was stunned. Surely this had not been orchestrated from the very beginning. But as it turned out, it had been carefully planned and executed. It was so effective that within a period of less than three weeks, it had disposed of a high-ranking executive who was earning a large portion of one department's payroll budget. It is a technique that seems best described by the phrase *bait and switch*.

Here Today, but Not Tomorrow

Jean was a truly talented manager. After spending years as a high school English teacher, she returned to graduate school in her mid-forties and earned a Ph.D. in organizational development. She then worked for some of New York City's best names in banking and management consulting. Those who worked with Jean knew her to be competent, exacting of her staff, and very thorough. Although not everyone with whom she worked was a fan, she did develop a loyal bond with several senior managers who benefited from her talents.

Jean's boss, Ron, an ambitious and determined director, was not one of her admirers. Put off by her intellect, threatened by her connections with top management, and fearing competition for a vice-presidential position, Ron decided he had to move her out of the way. Caught between an admiring top brass and Jean's own superior job performance, there appeared not much that he could do—that is, not until he heard about the pending hiring freeze.

Ron moved quickly. He called Jean into his office, showered her with praise and compliments, and told her that because she had done such a stellar job, he had created a new position for her. She would now be in charge of all executive development, succession, and consulting. This was the job of a lifetime, and despite the fact that she questioned Ron's motives, she couldn't help but accept the promotion.

Once again, Ron acted with expediency. He hired a replacement for Jean's old position before she even vacated it—so Jean could train the newcomer before she moved into the new position, he said. Two weeks went by before Jean heard from Ron again. Then the call came.

"Have you packed your office yet?" Ron inquired. When Jean said that she had, he told her to clear her schedule for the day and come down to his office. After she arrived in his office, Ron told Jean that he had made a terrible mistake: He hadn't gotten proper approval for the new position before he offered it to her; now a hiring freeze was in place, and there was no possibility of getting the new position approved. To put her back in the old job would be far too disruptive to the staff and the organization at large. Regrettably, the new position, a position she had never really occupied, had been eliminated. She was out of a job.

Ron had already covered his back with his boss, the vice president. He had explained his mistake, asked for forgiveness, and then proceeded to show how his mistake had reduced the department payroll significantly by eliminating the highest-paid staff member. It wasn't long before his boss was seeing the wisdom of Ron's "mistake."

Ron sent the usual sorry-to-see-you-go memo out and held an appropriate going-away luncheon. It was a terrible loss, he intoned with his eyes cast low, but times were tough and there was nothing that could be done. Jean, the story went, would be pursuing other interests. What he didn't say was that he had restored his eminence and cleared his path to the vice-presidential suite.

This kind of bait-and-switch routine has many derivatives. It is most useful when the targeted person is established and performing well in a job. The solution lies in moving the person to another job. By giving the employee a job that doesn't exist, as in the case of Jean, the employee can be quietly placed into an easily eliminated position. The same effect can be created by giving an employee a job that isn't what it appears to be, as in the case of Bryan.

Raise the Bar

Bryan was a purchasing manager for a large clothing manufacturer. Having been in his position for six years, he was well established and a strong performer. Everyone in manufacturing and engineering knew and liked Bryan. He wasn't overly bright, but he was always helpful and attentive to details, and he knew how to make the system work.

Bryan's new boss wasn't from the purchasing department. A demoted manager from product development, he was determined to regain his status by "turning around" the purchasing department. For whatever reasons, he decided that meant Bryan had to go.

Bryan's boss had worked with a particularly difficult and sticky area of purchasing when he had been in the Far East product development office during an earlier assignment. It was the job of currency exchange and foreign market procurement. With foreign exchange rates changing daily, the job was a nightmare. It would be perfect for Bryan, he decided.

Bryan was promoted into the job and within three months quit the company. He wasn't equipped for the demands of the job: He didn't speak any of the languages, wasn't familiar with product development, and was extremely unhappy at having to live overseas.

To say that Bryan's resignation was his choice—that he could have stuck it out and "paid his dues"—is absolutely true. What makes his leaving a singular layoff is that his layoff was engineered from the beginning. Bryan's boss had put him in a position knowing that Bryan would sink. The bar had been raised just beyond Bryan's reach. Fearing for his career record and realizing his deficiencies, Bryan left rather than face what he considered would be an eventual firing.

There are many other ways to push employees out without firing them; some of these devious techniques are set out in Exhibit 3. The point is this: Single targeted employees are laid off all the time for reasons that have nothing to do with their job performance or future potential.

Layoffs at the Top

Most of these one-on-one layoffs occur at the upper levels of the organization. Senior managers—directors and vice presidents—spend years climbing the corporate ladder to reach their positions. Most of them didn't get there because they were lazy or incompetent or insubordinate. As a group, they have worked diligently to earn the title and corner office, so when it comes time to push one of them out the door, it is generally difficult to do it for performance or competency reasons. Besides, most of these players are politically connected, and any overt attempt to oust them could be intercepted by one of their fellow executive

Exhibit 3. One-on-one execution techniques.

Bait and Switch

1. Promise the employee a newly created, more desirable position.
2. Replace the employee in his or her current job.
3. Fail to get funding for the new position, change the position to something much less than promised, or eliminate the new position before it ever really gets started.

Raise the Bar

1. Raise the performance standards of the job to a level that may exceed the skills of the employee.
2. Promise the employee support and resources to meet the new standards.
3. Have the employee agree to the new standards in writing.
4. Fail to deliver the promised help.
5. Severely decrease the employee's performance rating/merit pay.
6. Encourage the employee to quit before getting fired/fire the employee for inadequate performance.

Reorganize

1. Redistribute the workload among employees in a manner that eliminates a job by dividing up its duties among other positions.
2. Lay off the "extra" employee.
3. After a brief period, hire another employee to take on tasks that were displaced when other employees took on the tasks of the employee previously laid off; or after a year or so, return to the old organization and rehire for the position previously eliminated.

Do Nothing, Please

1. Create a position that has bogus duties.
2. Move the employee into the new position.
3. Eliminate the position and lay off the employee on the basis of "no value-added."

Impossible Dream

1. Create a new position that has seemingly reasonable expectations but cannot be met due to hidden factors (factors that are preferably in control of the manager); or make the employee dependent on the work of two other employees who can never agree or get along.

(continued)

Exhibit 3. Continued.

2. Severely reduce the performance rating/merit pay of the employee.
3. Encourage the employee to quit before getting fired/fire the employee for inadequate performance.

Cut Benefits

1. Reduce or eliminate the employee's benefit package. This is particularly effective with single parents who rely heavily on company-sponsored health care benefits.
2. Wait for the employee to quit.

Rescope the Job

1. Have the human resources department analyze the job (based heavily on your input).
2. When the decision is made to lower the pay scale for the job, have the employee "red-lined" so that he or she won't be eligible for pay raises for the foreseeable future.
3. Wait for the employee to quit.

Boss from Hell

1. Move the employee to a position under a boss who is known to be impossible.
2. Privately feed the new boss your concerns about the employee's performance and ability to do the job.
3. Wait for the blowup.

Slow Death

1. Consistently reinterpret everything that the employee does as mediocre or inferior.
2. Reward other employees in the department for equivalent performance.
3. Wait for the employee to quit.

Early Retirement

1. Strongly recommend that the employee take early retirement.
2. Blame the situation on another executive who "has it out" for the employee.
3. Tell the employee, "Get out while you can still get something."

Behind Closed Doors (Threats)

1. Privately threaten the employee with an impending firing if he or she doesn't quit.
2. Tell the employee you are providing an opportunity to avoid a bad mark on his or her record. If the person doesn't quit, it will only be a matter of time before he or she is fired.
3. Wait for the employee to quit.

Total Withdrawal

1. Completely withdraw from the employee. Refuse all meetings.
2. Withhold critical information the employee needs for success.
3. Wait for the employee to trip up or quit.

Dead-End Contract

1. Convince the employee of the benefits of becoming an external contractor (work at home, set your own hours, make more money, work for many companies, etc.).
2. Promise to hire the person for all the work he or she does now.
3. Once the employee resigns permanent employment status, fail to return phone calls, never sign a contract, never hire him or her for work.

---

supporters. Only in rare cases—usually during times of dreadful company performance—are senior executives fired.

Consequently, one-on-one techniques work well with the corporate upper echelon. In fact, this sort of cat-and-mouse political maneuvering is expected by most executives. They spend a fair amount of energy making sure their backs are protected at all times. When one has the misfortune of losing, it is simply accepted as a casualty of the game.

For those who know these rules and accept them, the one-on-one layoff isn't particulary damaging. Sure it hurts, but it is understood that what happened isn't necessarily personal and that future employers will know that too.

Damage of the One-on-One Execution

For those who didn't sign up for this game of career roulette—the ones who thought that showing up every day and doing a good job was enough—the one-on-one execution can be more devastating and undermining of confidence than an outright firing. When an employee is fired, almost everyone, including the employee, anticipates it before the actual event. Employees know when they aren't performing up to standard, and unless they are extremely dense, they see the growing frustration in the boss's face every day.

When an employee is forced out, it is not always obvious that a one-on-one layoff technique has been used. Usually only after the deed is done does it dawn on them what really happened, and they become shocked and angry. They thought they were doing a good job—really accomplishing something—and then suddenly they have had their job snatched out from under them. They are denied the answers to crucial questions like "Was it something I did?" and "Why didn't you just tell me, and I could have changed it?"

Sometimes there is a rash of one-on-one layoffs throughout the organization, most commonly when a no-nonsense manager comes to power and issues the command to purge the workforce of slackers, sluggards, and such. Managers who have already been riding close herd have little choice but to single out an otherwise fine employee for sacrifice. Not to respond to the call for purge reflects badly on the manager's performance. Such inaction might mean he or she doesn't have what it takes to make tough management calls.

The one-on-one layoff serves some compelling political needs within the organization. It completely subverts the performance management process and consequently avoids all the hassles of firing based on performance and the bad press of a layoff. Devalued employees are pushed silently out the back door and left to pick up the pieces with little help from their now ex-employer. This type of layoff can be the most psychologically and financially devastating of any of the layoffs, especially when it comes in the form of a forced resignation.

7

Human Resources as the Corporate KGB

The ability to deal with people is as purchasable a commodity as sugar or coffee. And I pay more for that ability than for any other under the sun.

John D. Rockefeller (1839–1937)

Where has the human resources (HR) department been during this wholesale massacre of the corporation's human assets? Why have they not intervened? Why have they not collected the abundant evidence that layoffs are undermining the company and spread it across the corporate boardroom for all the decision makers to see? What about all of the carnage of morale and loyalty that is left in shambles after the deed is done? Why is it that these professionals, the same ones who must try to put the pieces back together after the fact, haven't protested the continued use of the layoff ax?

There are a variety of viewpoints on why HR departments haven't been more active in deterring the layoff craze. One of the more satirical views comes from Jerry B. Harvey at George Washington University, who wrote a part-serious, part-humorous "sermon" titled "Eichmann in the Organization" in which he likens many of the HR professionals to Adolf Eichmann. Eichmann, the Jewish bureaucrat who cooperated with the Nazis, was responsible for uncountable deaths among the Jewish businessmen who trusted and confided in him.

Others support the layoff movement and feel HR is not doing enough to pare down the workforce. They suggest that

HR should have been leading the charge to discard workers all along. In fact, according to this view, it was HR that created much of the problem in the first place by having inadequate controls on hiring and ineffective means of managing employee performance. Skyrocketing benefit costs and highly paid employees who do precious little for the organization all point to a department lulled into a bureaucratic trance. Enlightened HR managers are helping their organizations to stick to the diet of no hiring and are proclaiming the benefits of being lean and mean.

A more reasonable understanding of HR's handling of the layoff movement can be found by a brief revisiting of the origins of the HR department. Historically, it was created as an extension of senior management. It had no real power on its own and functioned to carry out the wishes of management and buffer management from some of the more uncomfortable labor issues. To a great extent, this remains true today.

The Rise of the Human Resources Department

The Early Years

By the late 1800s, the industrial revolution was in full swing. In the wake of modernizing and automating, a widening economic chasm developed between the owners and the managers of the factories. The laborers, many immigrants to the cities from the farms, were extremely poor and lived in largely unsanitary conditions. Child labor and abusive labor practices were rampant, creating a dissatisfied and neglected workforce ripe for unionization. Enter the welfare secretary.

Welfare secretaries were positions created in turn-of-the-century corporations to fulfill two purposes: stave off the move to unionize, and create an incentive to make appreciative workers work even longer hours. These secretaries helped employees with personal problems such as education, housing, and medical needs. To some extent, these forerunners to the personnel specialist also worked to improve working conditions by advocating the addition of washup facilities, locker rooms, lunch-rooms, and recreational facilities for workers.

By the 1920s, however, welfare work in industry had declined and become somewhat discredited. Some companies operated their programs in a highly paternalistic manner and continued them only as long as the workers evidenced genuine appreciation. Other employers offered these benefits to their employees in exchange for accepting long hours, low wages, and bad working conditions. In short, the failure of the welfare movement to increase plant productivity resulted in the demise of the welfare secretary position.

The period between 1910 and World War I saw the beginnings of the first real personnel function. Because of the popularity of Frederick Taylor's scientific management approach and its emphasis on proper selection of employees, the field of employment management evolved. The employment manager's job was to assist in hiring employees who were capable of meeting very specific requirements for jobs. This gave the personnel function its first real contribution to the organization: hiring employees who could perform jobs efficiently and safely.

With the passage of workers' compensation laws, safely became an increasingly important (and expensive) issue. In fact, legislation regarding worker safety led to the creation of much of the personnel, or human resources, department as we now know it. The employment agent, the company doctor or nurse, the safety director, and the training director were all created to hire, oversee, and train safety among the laborers.

Legal Compliance and Buffering

During the Great Depression, many citizens lost faith in the ability of business to meet society's needs. Instead, they turned to government, which intervened to give workers unemployment compensation, social security, minimum wages, and the federally protected right to join a union. Almost all of these programs required company contributions, monitoring, and extensive record keeping.

Coupled with an exponentially growing tide of unionization, companies raced to beef up personnel departments with clerks to administer programs designed to comply with the law and deter unionization. Labor relations positions were created in the department to deal with negotiating labor contracts. Compensation clerks were hired to conduct surveys to make sure that the labor contract wages were comparable to those of other companies. By the 1950s, the personnel department had grown to be one of the largest staff functions in the corporation.

These departments were charged with keeping workers satisfied, out of unions, and productive. Management largely abdicated responsibility for personnel policies and decisions to the personnel department, which created the convenient and much overly used excuse: "There's nothing I can do about it. Go talk to Personnel." Company management no longer had to deal with the potentially volatile issues of salary and promotion, and the personnel department became the buffer between management and labor.

Enter the Behavioral Sciences

During the recessions of the seventies and eighties, management began looking to personnel to contribute more than just the legal compliance and buffering functions. With more and more economic pressure on companies, management began to devolve to the personnel department responsibility for improving and streamlining the workforce. Large numbers of behavioral scientists joined the ranks of Personnel during this period, eager to contribute their knowledge of skill and performance assessment. The behavioral science methodology required the tracking of all manner of individual performance data. Assessment centers, skills testing, structured interviews, and behaviorally anchored performance instruments, to name a few, were introduced to the corporation as methods for refining and improving the performance of the workforce.

Since the mid-1980s, senior management has continually looked to HR for assistance in choosing the names for a layoff. The well-educated and psychometrically equipped behavioral scientists leaped at the opportunity to employ their skills. In large part, it was felt that determining company strategy was the responsibility of senior management; the HR department was responsible for attaining the objectives handed to it with the greatest expertise and efficiency. Hence, these behavioral scientists went to work in choosing the "right" names for the layoff, without challenging the overall strategy.

Behavioral science done correctly requires lots of objective data about the subjects it examines. Good behavioral scientists know that the only way to make accurate predictions about future behavior is to know as much as possible about past behavior. Sound data require many observations from several different observers in a variety of performance situations. In other words, the more that is known about an employee's past behavior patterns, the better are the decisions about hiring, promotion, and compensation. Sometimes knowing personal information like credit history and mental illness can greatly enhance predictions about trustworthiness, stability, and honesty.

As a result, well-meaning HR departments have become the internal clearinghouses of information about the employees of the organization. Within its tightly controlled walls are locked rooms of file cabinets that contain the official and legally compliant personnel files—and other cabinets with jucier, more "politically" relevant information. Within these cherished folders are collections of performance reviews, applications for employment, interview notes, letters of reprimand, reasons for demotions or denial of promotions, assessments of future potential, possible future positions, and notes regarding health and disability. And all of that is just what is in writing.

Inside those closed-door conference rooms are personnel specialists who are called upon by senior managers to make all kinds of decisions regarding personnel and careers. Human resources employees regularly determine how much to pay employees, which employees should be promoted, who should be fired, who should be granted leaves of absence, and who should be offered early retirement. These walking sponges absorb information wherever they might find it: in the lunchroom, from an overheard phone conversation, during a company outing, from supervisors, coworkers, suppliers, and customers. The truly effective HR person knows his or her "people" and is willing to offer advice and summary judgments on demand.

Sound more like a fictionalized story about J. Edgar Hoover's FBI than your company? Well, take a closer look. I have been part of several HR departments and consulted to dozens more. Without exception, every time I part the veil of good intentions and I'm-a-people-person attitude I find a department that functions in large part as the centralized intelligence center for the corporation. A few years ago, I observed a human resources department with a particularly brutal method for processing all of this employee information. Here's what I saw.

The Corporate War Room

The drive west from Newark Airport to Basking Ridge, New Jersey, changed everything I had believed to be true about New Jersey. We passed through beautiful rolling hills with small farms nestled next to serene ponds and the occasional misfit mansion and golf course on our way to the AT&T corporate headquarters. When we arrived, I was again surprised and, I must say, a bit disappointed at the lack of grandeur that usually accompanies buildings of such corporate eminence. With not a car or parking lot in sight, we pulled into a graciously understated, tile-roofed building whose first floor revealed an enormous parking garage. Once inside, the seeming miles of corridors we traversed made it clear that this was indeed the epitome of understated, gargantuan architecture. Had it not been for the occasional unique art piece that punctuated the rows of identical white offices, I would have been completely lost.

We arrived at the human resources department. Our host, Vicki, an HR executive, led us to a door that appeared on the outside to be identical to the hundred or more white doors we had passed on our trip from the garage. She unlocked and opened the door with an airtight swish, revealing a warm room filled with a rich mahogany table surrounded with generously padded, high-back armchairs. Two of the four walls were large picture windows that looked out onto the rolling green lawns and manicured gardens, and on the other two walls hung large mahogany panels, evenly spaced, and each with large, shiny brass locks in the middle.

Once we were all seated around the table, Vicki began the presentation many of us had flown across the country to see. We were corporate managers of succession planning (the process of planning for future job incumbents through internal promotion) for large companies across the United States and had been invited to view AT&T's succession planning process. Before getting into the meat of the presentation, Vicki filled us in on a few of the details of the affectionately labeled "war room" where we were sitting.

"The windows have been coated with a special film that cannot be seen through from the outside during either the night or the day," she pointed out as she drummed her manicured nails on the pane. "The walls of the room have lead sheeting, and a special white-noise sound-masking system prevents any sound from leaving the room," she said as she held her finger to her lips so that we would be aware of the low din of sound coming from somewhere within the ceiling. "You can never be too careful," she admonished, rapping on the solid metal door. "The information in this room must be protected and remain only in the hands of the decision makers.

"Access to this room is e-x-t-r-e-m-e-l-y limited. Only the CEO, top executives, and the occasional visitor like yourselves are allowed to use it. I have one full-time person on my staff whose job is to monitor its use and to maintain the information in the room. We don't even allow caterers to serve coffee or lunch during long meetings. We meet them at the door and serve it ourselves."

Vicki and her assistant then inserted keys into the brass locks on the mahogany paneled walls and swung them open to reveal something that I tongue-in-cheek describe as the corporate refrigerator. (Remember how important the outside of the refrigerator door was when you were little? All those brightly colored magnets held special pictures of proud grandparents, good report cards, and special awards.) What these mahogany panels had hidden from view were large boards covered with hundreds of magnets, two by four inches, with the picture, name, and title of every managing executive in the company, all arranged in a hierarchical organization chart. With the panel doors open, we were surrounded on two sides by hundreds of black-and-white photo magnets staring back at us.

The magnets were arranged in Christmas-tree-style formations, with each tree representing one of the various businesses of AT&T International. For the most part they were neatly lined up according to the reporting structures, with the exception of a dozen or so that seemed to be intentionally turned on a 45-degree diagonal and a few that were scattered about the sidelines. Curiously, some magnets had red dots and some green dots pasted to their front. Anxious to learn all we could, we began firing questions at our articulate host.

As it turns out, those magnets placed on the diagonal were managers whose careers were, shall we say, in transition. These were the executives whose future would most likely hold a move—perhaps a promotion, or a transfer, or, in the worst case, a layoff. For whatever reasons, however, the jury was still out on these executives, and their future with the company was yet to be determined.

The significance of the red and green dots had a greater ring of finality. "Those with a green sticker have earned the corporate 'star on the forehead' and are awaiting a promotion while those with a red sticker are slated for termination," Vicki said matter-of-factly.

Silence prevailed. The fact that all of these careers were reduced to magnets with little mug shots that could be moved about or even discarded on a whim had a chilling effect. It's not that any of us hadn't dealt with the same facts of corporate life many times before; rather, there was something mesmerizing about scanning the walls and looking the red-dotted photos in the eye, knowing that soon the day would come when they would learn that their future would be dramatically different from their own plan. How long had they worked for the company, scratching their way up to an executive position? Were they complete idiots and just no longer cutting it? Did they have children in college? Had they given up their personal and social lives to move to parts unknown at the company's bidding?

Vicki filled the silence: "The data displayed on these walls are invaluable. The CEO and his staff will sometimes hold all-day meetings in here mapping out 'what-if' scenarios. Sometimes at the end of the day they will have moved all the pieces around . . . and they have to mark which pieces should stay and which should return to their current position. Other times they will come in and ventilate," she said as she randomly discarded magnets from the board. "Our CEO feels it helps sometimes to simply make some room for new blood."

The concept of ventilating was new to me. Vicki explained that it happened when a particular area of the business was getting stale—perhaps not growing as expected or not earning the revenues sought. The CEO or a staff member would examine the board and pull off names in places where the fresh breeze of new talent and ideas might get things going again. Vicki suggested that the person who is "ventilated" in the process may have had a good track record but would be sacrificed to make room for the stimulus to push the business forward.

Gazing out the window, I noticed the lush lawn that seemed to flow over the gentle hills surrounding the building we were in. It took me back to my childhood in the ever so gently flowing cotton fields of northern Louisiana. My own Uncle Bill lived in a small farming community among those cotton growers and had worked for what in those days we simply knew as the "phone company." My family spent holidays with Uncle Bill and his family, and I often remember his being called out in the night or in the middle of a dinner to answer a call for phone service repair. Even when his own home was destroyed by a tornado and his mother-in-law thrown hundreds of feet from the house and critically injured, he was back on the job within hours, doing everything he could to get the phone service back in order.

But as happened with many others, the day came when Uncle Bill was forced to take early retirement. My aunt went back to work to help with the mortgage, and Uncle Bill took on some contract work and a school bus route to make up the difference. Life had always been tough for my uncle and aunt; now, being too old to start over and living among lifelong friends in a rural economy that was devastated, they had little choice but to buckle down, cut back, and do what they could to survive.

I wondered if the decision that forced Uncle Bill's retirement had been the fallout of someone's "ventilating." Perhaps it had been a bad day in the war room. Had someone needed to show that he or she had the "mettle" to make hard decisions? Maybe not. Maybe it just made good business sense to offer early retirement to a group of excess, aging telephone repairmen. Whatever or however the decision was made, I was sinking deep in my overstuffed chair feeling the weight of responsibility on the decisions made in this room. Were those who gathered about this table to decide the fate of so many going about the work with genuine respect and compassion? I hoped so.

The rest of our visit went swiftly as we were given stacks of sample forms that are used to run the AT&T succession planning process. An hour and a half after entering, we were ushered out of the war room to another important meeting. We were again led down indeterminable lengths of corridors into a beautifully appointed, atrium cafeteria, where we sat and mulled over what we had just seen.

After conducting other business, I returned to my hotel room that evening with the war room still very much on my mind. I was fascinated and troubled by what I had seen—troubled that a few executives had so much power over so many careers. The cold, gaming quality of that room rubbed my already callused sensitivity in these matters raw, and yet I knew there was nothing malicious or intentionally evil about it. All it really did was bring into plain view the backroom discussions that I knew have always determined corporate successions. Those "black market" talent deals made among allied executives over martinis are usually far more objectionable than anything I had seen in the war room that day. Whether I liked it or not, the war room simply collected the reins of power into one central command.

Layoffs and the War Room

When layoffs are the order of the day, the war room of any company becomes extremely busy—so busy that, besides legal compliance and record keeping, it becomes the sole focus of HR.

Planning and conducting a layoff is immense and takes

months of work. With so many HR departments cut to the bone themselves through layoffs, every hand is needed to carry off the next round of firings with finesse. It is common among HR professionals who entered the workforce since the mid-1980s to have orchestrated many layoffs. For some, that is all they have ever done; they are layoff specialists. One particularly seasoned HR manager who worked in high-tech companies told me she had personally laid off more than 3,000 employees.

With so much demand, there is little time for these professionals to rethink some of their methods. Their attention focuses on the details of execution, not on the validity of the decisions being made. Are the employees who are slated for layoffs really excess staff or just misplaced staff? Is critical knowledge going out the door with those who are dismissed? More important, how will we put the pieces back together after the layoff?

Still, the emphasis is on the actual firings. Company communications are written and rewritten, until they are innocuous, albeit meaningless, messages. Scripts for managers are pored over and examined for accuracy and protection against litigation. Up until the last minute, schedules are compiled and recompiled; severance packages printed; conference rooms with security guards reserved. Then there is the question of what to tell the remaining employees. Do we say nothing? (Many companies do just that.) Do we give the survivors pay raises and pats on the back to help salvage morale? What do we tell customers? Suppliers? The list of details that we must attend to is almost endless.

There is much talk in the HR world about becoming a "business partner" and being more "strategic." The reality is that the demands of laying off employees have drained any energy that might have been channeled toward strategic planning in the HR department. Senior management has grown accustomed to using HR staff as hatchet men—someone to turn to for action, not ideas, and certainly not for resistance. The real value that HR adds to the company, in the minds of most senior managers, is to make sure paychecks go out, benefits are distributed, and employee information is maintained.

The Corporate Conscience Myth

Some human resources professionals like to think of their department as a sort of corporate conscience. These good-intentioned specialists see the HR department as representing humanistic values in the corporate decision process. Their mission is to protect the interests of employees while executing the wishes of management.

This idealized parental role is in direct conflict with the demands placed on HR by management. Take, for example, Dave, a purchasing manager for a large company with which I consulted. In his mid-forties, Dave was going through something of a midlife crisis. With the breakup of his marriage and problems with a teenage child, coupled with the malaise that comes with having done the same job for eleven years, Dave was questioning some of his life decisions. Thinking that his HR representative was someone who would understand, he made an appointment to discuss the possibility of a career change within the company. Assuming that the HR representative had his best interests at heart and would keep their conversation confidential, Dave spilled out his frustrations in the meeting. Unknown to Dave at the time, his company was planning a layoff the next week.

Behind the scenes, all of the HR representatives were meeting with senior managers to confirm their list of employees to be laid off. When the HR representative met with Dave's manager, Dave's name came up with phrases like, "I'm not sure about his commitment to the company" and "Perhaps he would be better off moving on to something else." Despite an excellent performance record, Dave found himself holding a pink slip the next week.

HR cannot play the role of corporate compliance *and* protector of employees. Those two roles clash and are at odds with one another. In almost every organization, HR success is measured by how well HR staff execute management decisions. Being the corporate conscience—the ballast that keeps the ship morally erect—doesn't do anything toward accomplishing this objective. In fact, it most often creates resistance and opposition to management decisions that are deemed to violate HR sensibilities.

While this role may be good for corporate etiquette, it doesn't show on the annual report. HR professionals who cling to this do-gooder model find themselves repeatedly bloodied, battered, and burned out.

HR departments play a critical role in the corporation, but it is not, as HR managers claim, one of strategic planning or power. The department is a staff function that has a long history of being the implementer, not the creator, of management decisions. HR ensures compliance with labor laws, fair compensation, tracking, and maintaining employee information, and it is a buffer between management and employees. Although the terms *internal covert intelligence officer* and *executioner* may be distasteful to all but the most unfeeling in HR, these are ongoing functions in the department. There is little argument with the fact that technically sophisticated HR professionals have changed the face of employment in America. Without them, the decisions to lay off millions of American workers by senior executives and boards of directors could have never been accomplished so quickly or easily.

Part Three

The Personal Cost of a Layoff: Pain and Recovery

The personal cost of a layoff only *starts* with the loss of a paycheck. The road beyond the dismissal is filled with financial and psychological obstacles that assault the newly unemployed at an ever increasing rate. If the former employee is mid-career or beyond, the toll of being laid off increases dramatically. Recovery from this career crisis is possible, but it takes time, effort, and courage. With some thought and planning beforehand, the potential victim of a layoff can protect himself or herself and minimize the ravaging effects.

In the first two chapters of Part Three, Camille Stogner writes about her experience of being laid off and her recovery. Chapter 10 takes a close look at the impact of a layoff on those who are hit hardest: older workers. Chapter 11 explores how to minimize the personal damage of a layoff.

8

Have a Great Vacation

by Camille Stogner

A Dream Come True

Vacation! The very thought sent waves of anticipation and excitement through my imagination. Vacation—an old-fashioned, go-on-a-trip, do-the-tourist-thing, be-with-family time. The first such vacation my husband, Jerry, and I had had in five years. Not a week to stay at home and paint the house or wax the floors, but an actual vacation. The day had arrived after six months of planning and years of being submerged in our individual careers and obligations without taking a real vacation. One of the best things about it was that everything was prepaid. I had nothing to worry about except having a good time. Leaving the hot, humid South for a week of beautiful weather in San Francisco seemed like a dream, and it was about to come true. The anticipated day had arrived, and our flight was scheduled to leave at 4:30 P.M.—the culmination of weeks of planning and late nights and early mornings at the office, all to get caught up for my one-week absence from the office. Vacation!

This vacation was well deserved after my nearly seven years of employment with Crawford and Company, a health and rehabilitation services company. As an RN, I had been hired as a medical services consultant for this international company and had quickly moved up the career ladder. I was in charge of the staff of the main branch and two satellite branches in other cities. My job required me to train and manage the employees in remote locations, and I frequently traveled. The job was a challenging one, due partly to the nature of the work and partly to

internal office politics. I had pride in my work and my reputation in the field.

The last five years had also been filled with new beginnings
in my personal life. Jerry and I had created and opened a retail
business: an audio and music store specializing in the design
and installation of professional sound equipment. Jerry had
worked and studied for many years to gain the necessary expertise and a credible reputation in the field, and the opening of the
store fulfilled his lifelong dream. After much careful planning,
we had poured all our resources into the store and weathered
the first year of his self-employment. During the first years, we
had anticipated no great financial rewards, instead funneling all
profits back into the business. We would rely on my income and
company benefits until the store became profitable.

Jerry and I love children and dreamed of having a family
together. Accepting the news that we would be unable to have
any on our own was particularly difficult, so we decided to pursue adopting an infant and made numerous applications to
adoption agencies. Well-meaning counselors who knew the dis-
couraging odds for adopting a newborn advised us, "Forget it
and get on with your lives."

Aside from being difficult and taking many years, adoption
is expensive. But we were determined and forged ahead, completing the various applications and enduring the interview
process. We lived our lives as though in a glass fishbowl while
we were examined, tested, looked at, and evaluated by agency
after agency. We joked that we would become grandparents before we ever got to be parents!

We had just built a new home, partly to enhance our qualifications for adoption but mostly so that we could have a nursery
in case the long-awaited call came. We hadn't yet sold our previous home, so every penny was tightly budgeted, and we were
totally dependent on two incomes.

But now these worries faded into the background as we prepared to leave for vacation. Thoughts of last-minute errands and
packing chased away any remaining thoughts of monthly reports, budgets, billable hours, and office politics. It was the kind
of feeling that nothing can put a damper on the day—that is,
until the ringing telephone jolted me out of reverie.

When the telephone rang, I was caught in a dilemma, trying to choose between a light-green jacket and a dark-blue sweater for the cool evenings in California. I was surprised to hear Delores, my boss for the past seven years. Begrudgingly I slipped back into work mode and tried to imagine what it was I might have left undone. It was then that I heard the news that would take my entire world and shatter it into a million pieces.

The Ax Falls

The words and flat tone of her voice are forever imprinted in my memory: "I need you to bring your company car, keys, and anything else that belongs to Crawford and Company to my office as soon as possible." My immediate reaction was shocked silence. Then, with a voice I could not identify as my own, I choked, "Can you tell me what is going on?" The jagged edges of the next few words assaulted my ears and tore at my gut: "I am laying you off, effective immediately. I have ordered your final paycheck, and I need you to come get your personal things from your office."

Pelted by the words and implications, I sat stunned for what seemed like hours. I repeated the words to myself over and over again, trying to make sense out of the situation, but none would surface. The words echoed as in a canyon: LAID OFF—LAID OFF—LAID OFF. No job. No paycheck. No health or life insurance for me and my husband. No company car and car insurance. Not being a part of the group anymore. An immediate cessation of the daily routine of the last seven years. No longer a vital part of the company. I was unnecessary, excess baggage. NOT GOOD ENOUGH.

My thoughts raced as my mind scrambled to search for some justification that this could not possibly be true. How could it? Recently I was honored by one of the company vice presidents and awarded the coveted Supervisor of the Year award, a highlight of my career. I had been employed in the local office longer than any other employee with the single exception of Delores, the branch manager. I had hired, trained, and supervised almost every employee in the branch. Additionally, I had twice been awarded the Employee of the Year award. I thought that my seniority would provide some shield should the poison-tipped layoff arrows ever start flying in my direction. Deliberately working to become a valuable employee, I was the person other employees, customers, and vendors called for guidance and answers to questions. I had consistently earned the highest performance ratings possible—a five out of a possible five. What I thought had been the reward of my contribution—the highest salary of any other employee at the same level—had become, as it turns out, a two-edged sword.

At the very core of the swirling, almost incoherent thoughts was the nagging question: What did I do that was so bad that they wanted to let me go?

As an almost desperate and self-protective measure, I kept pushing that mocking question away and assuring myself that I had nothing to do with my firing. I had been a truly dedicated employee. I had been my manager's right hand for years. Together we had faced many personnel problems, including hiring and firing and, yes, laying people off. We had weathered some lean and unprofitable years as we gradually built up a solid staff and had recently earned some handsome profits, for which we would both begin to benefit through bonus programs. Delores had told me repeatedly, "If you were ever to leave this company, I could never run this place without you. You have made this office the profitable office that it is today." I had covered for her by troubleshooting, preparing reports, handling administrative problems that arose, and being available to the staff because Delores frequently was out of the office. I had gone far beyond my own job description during her absences. She reciprocated by giving me the independence and freedom to do my job as I thought best. Through good months and bad, we shared camaraderie and friendship. We always looked for the humor when times were tough, and by sharing a few laughs together, we made both our jobs a little easier. Our relationship was one that I would come to greatly miss.

As my mind raced back, it stopped on the memory of a conversation I had recently had with Delores. It had troubled me at the time, but I had pushed it away because it did not really pertain to me, or so I thought. She had told me about the circumstances surrounding the sudden disappearance of a manager from the corporate roster. It was generally known that this manager was hardworking and had substantial skill and expertise in her field. She had been successful in her position for a period of years and had recently experienced some personal problems at home and with her health. Suddenly she was no longer around. Delores told me that the regional manager called her departure a necessary action because, he said, "she has served her purpose." Those words haunted me for days as I pondered the unthinkable: Had I simply served my purpose now that profits were up? Surely there must be some mistake. Crawford and Company would never be so cruel.

Suddenly I visualized the Supervisor of the Year award ceremony. The regional director and vice president gave a flattering speech about me to the group prior to presenting the award. We listened to him as he told of my accomplishments, one after the other. Winking in my direction, he told the group, "Do not think that we [upper management] do not know who is responsible for turning the office around and making it profitable." He gushed on about the difficult circumstances that I had labored under, that my commitment and dedication were rare qualities, and that the company was so fortunate to have me on the team. How empty and fake those words sounded to me now as they echoed in my brain.

Departing Shots

As I entered the familiar office for the final time, I realized that I had already, by virtue of the unspoken rules of the game, become an outcast, an outsider, an adversary, the *enemy*. I was learning a chilling lesson about what I had believed to be a warm and caring company. In the not so distant past, I had repeatedly told prospective employees that Crawford and Company stood apart from the rest of the corporate world in the way it treated employees. I now knew I had unknowingly sold a bill of counterfeit goods. My own words haunted me: "Crawford and Company always stands behind its people . . . takes care of employees . . . treats everyone with nurturing and protective warmth."

The dance we did as Delores and I tiptoed around my numbed ambivalence and her obvious feelings of guilt made the short visit brutal. She told me that she was only following orders from the regional office, against her wishes, due to a recent slump in business. She begged me not to go, while she handed me a form to sign regarding COBRA (health insurance for the unemployed). She told me to stay, while also saying that it was going to be difficult to handle the office without my assistance. She held out her hand for the keys to my company car as she told me that she would work something out for me to stay. She indicated that this would all blow over, while she told me that she would miss me terribly. She was in tears as she told me to go on my vacation; when I returned, she would have the entire matter "straightened out." In the manner of a consolation prize, she told me that the manager in a branch located two and a half hours away was in need of some part-time help. Of course, I wouldn't qualify for a company car; the five-hour daily commute would be on my own time; no guarantees would be made about how many hours a week I would be working; and I probably would not qualify for health insurance or any other benefits. But with a positive gesture, she offered to make the telephone call to "assist" me in obtaining that job. Thanks for the offer, I blurted out, but no thanks.

With all the mixed messages, I wasn't sure whether I was actually laid off. I knew that I had signed a form, but I was not given a final paycheck or any certainty as to when to expect one. When I tried to get some things from my office, she told me not to, that would indicate such finality, and she would not be able to stand it.

After I handed over my keys, hurriedly packed a few boxes, and raked my desktop into my briefcase, I walked out with my heavy eyelids straining to hold back the onslaught of tears. That short trip down the familiar, once comfortable hallways and to the parking lot lasted a lifetime. Delores's words were ringing in my soul: "Don't take this personally; it is just a business decision. Go on and try to HAVE A NICE VACATION." The faces of co-workers masked with helpless smiles still loom in my memory. Were they truly helpless, or were they co-conspirators? Was it genuine empathy I saw flash in their eyes, or merely gratitude that they had been spared? Those minutes while I left the office for the last time are lost in the blur of my own efforts to stay composed and retain some dignity as I walked away from a major part of my life with only a few hours' notice.

Then the enormity of it all hit me. How would we ever qualify for an adoption without my income? How would we pay for the new house? Where would we find affordable health insurance? The frustration began to boil. This decision made in a distant boardroom was destroying *my* life and *my* family. What right had these people to intrude upon my life and, in one swift move, dash our dreams?

As we boarded the plane later that day, I became acutely aware of the buzz of conversation and business lingo spilling around me. Professional men and women were comfortably sharing stories, ideas, and schedules. The stinging realization that I was no longer a part of that corporate club was more than I could bear. I gratefully accepted earphones from the flight attendant and pretended to watch a movie, so I could have the privacy to nurse my wounds. Just yesterday I felt I was a vital part of the business world, with something to offer it. Today I felt useless and thrown away, as though I had "served my purpose" for the company.

The Aftermath

My vacation did not do what a vacation is intended to do, but it did give me an opportunity to do some serious soul searching and fit the puzzle pieces together. Although Delores's ambivalence made me uncertain whether the layoff decision was final, I nevertheless felt extremely vulnerable. Every time a new wave of realization washed over me, I was left with an ache. The searing pain of rejection was almost too painful to bear. I tried not to become consumed by the financial implications as I toured the beautiful city and countryside with the "I am OK" mask firmly in place. Very naively, perhaps stupidly, I hoped and even expected that if the layoff was final, the company would surely offer a decent severance agreement after so many years of faithful employment. What a disillusionment!

By the time we returned home, I was no closer to identifying a course of action than when we left. When I picked up the mail from the week, the absolute crowning blow was delivered. Peeking out from between routine bills and advertisements was a warmly colored, inviting brochure. As I pulled it from the stack and read it, I became enraged. The brochure was the monthly newsletter sent out by my employer, entitled *The Crawford Family*, and filled to capacity with heartwarming stories of the ways Crawford and Company takes care of employees and families. It oozed with statistics on how profitable a year the company was enjoying.

Thus began the long and arduous healing process.

The first few weeks were devoted to taking care of business, including determining whether I had actually been laid off. I was disabled by the lack of finality of my "exit interview." I was unsure whether to look for a job or try to return to my old job. We knew that we had to establish some income quickly in order to maintain our living expenses and continue the health insurance. Moreover, we had to make some transportation arrangements now that I no longer had the company car.

One of my first bitter doses of reality came when my telephone calls to the company were not returned, and I sensed a distinctive difference in the way the receptionist spoke to me. The usual upbeat, friendly voice lowered an octave and became hushed and very serious when she recognized my voice. Of the several people I spoke to, no one seemed to know what to say, but all seemed in a sudden hurry to pass the call on to someone else. How I longed to cry out, "It is just me! The one you used to have fun with and talk to. I have not changed. I am still the same person." But I never did. Rejection compounded rejection until I knew something had to change or I would be completely destroyed by this situation. My questions regarding my employment had been answered without any words from management. I was put in the position to have to beg for any crumb of well-deserved severance that might be thrown my way. What an ending!

The coldness that met me as I attempted to get some response from the regional director and the company attorney was infuriating. These people with whom I had been on friendly terms only a few weeks ago, now treated me like an uninvited salesperson. They had nothing to say to me and no longer needed to offer friendliness. That obvious change of attitude seemed to invalidate all the years of our upbeat, professional working relationship. Had the entire seven years been one big facade?

After several weeks of silence, the telephone began to ring with well wishes from the friends I had made on the job. These were strained conversations at best, but nonetheless I was appreciative they made the effort. Eventually I did receive calls from Delores. She would ramble on about problems at work and how she wished I was there to help solve them. After several such telephone calls I decided to close this chapter and move on with my life. Whatever I did with my career at this point would be better than what I was doing to myself by allowing this abuse to continue.

During the next weeks and months I endured some devasting experiences (described in the next chapter), but my story does not end here.

A Fresh Start

A major shift in direction came unexpectedly one day when I was contacted by a friend who is an attorney. When he called, he did not know that I had been laid off. He began talking to me about a malpractice case that he was working on and asked my opinion about some of the medical issues. Before we ended the conversation, he had hired me as a medical-legal consultant for that particular case and suggested that I go into business as an independent consultant, with his promise of more future business. I was stunned by the idea. I certainly had been well trained and educated to do that kind of work, but we already had one self-employed person in the family, and I was not eager to jump on that train. However, after a little research, I discovered that there was not very much competition for this kind of consulting service in my area. Even more enticing, I knew that I could successfully compete with my ex-employer in this arena.

This idea, simultaneously terrifying and exciting, began to

evolve. Soon afterward, our spare bedroom became an office, a brand-new occupational license hung on the wall, and a full box of business cards beckoned from the wobbly desk. Using all my years of corporate experience and training, I was officially in business as a medical-legal consultant with a single client.

Two months from the day that I was officially laid off, I picked up the ringing telephone and heard the adoption counselor say, "I have good news!" Our exultation over the possibility of having our long-awaited family was quickly tempered by doubt and uncertainty because of our financial status. We feared that we could not legally qualify as adoptive parents due to the loss of income. We faced the probability of staggering adoption expenses, plus the cost of taking care of an infant. Thus, we embarked on another journey of uncertainty, but one that had such a happy ending.

With grit and determination, we persisted in seeking new business to bring in the additional income. The office lights started burning at all hours of the night and continue now, while our son is asleep. We sold anything of value that we could to defray the adoption expenses. I became accustomed to driving a temperamental car, badly in need of repair. Jerry worked days, nights, weekends, and holidays to increase the business. Together as a family, we have pushed and pulled through one of the most difficult times of our lives.

My office now has all varieties of toys scattered between the files and the executive coffee cup. As I watch our beautiful baby grow, I know that everything has worked out for the best in spite of the trauma. We have moved forward, looking back only to measure the progress. It is one of those bittersweet lessons in life that we love to hate.

9

Falling Down
by Camille Stogner

Trading Places

For a newly laid-off employee, the first visit to the unemployment office can be a humbling experience. Something happens to you between the pink slip and the unemployment line. All comfortable identity is stripped away, leaving a vulnerable and less-than-confident shadow of times past. Yesterday you were an Important Person with a job, and you belonged to a group—a group that consists of people who, like yourself, take responsibility seriously, endure long hours, and sacrifice to help bring home the bacon. A group that works together, solves problems together, eats together, celebrates members' birthdays together, endures boring seminars together, pretends to enjoy Christmas parties and company picnics together, shares personal problems together, and enjoys a common bond. To that group, you no longer belong. Now the most critical decision to make is which line to stand in to sign up for unemployment—alone.

In this new group, the pecking order is established solely on the basis of who has been standing in line the longest. For hours you sit and stand in a stifling room decorated with faded posters lined with prison bars and authoritative warnings to those who would attempt to defraud the system. Processed like a bunch of cows en route to the slaughterhouse, you follow the painted green arrows mutely from one desk to another, answering questions, filling out forms, feeling the acute sting of each inquiry why you lost your job. You know that you are entitled to the benefits, but shame floods your mind as you apply for financial assistance behind an invisible sign that reads, "Beggars stand here."

There is very little casual conversation here. Everyone seems to be enveloped in their own struggles, and no one seems to be in a hurry. A few diehards still clutch their briefcases with white knuckles, as though letting go signifies acceptance of their plight. People from all economic levels and educational backgrounds are represented here, most looking shell-shocked. It is probably one of the few places where such a diversified group comes together in unity for the same cause. Suddenly all economic, educational, language, racial, and sexual barriers dissipate as we nurse our individual and collective wounds. There is little comfort in knowing that you are not in this alone. "Let go," "kicked out," "shown the door," "restructured," "reorganized," "downsized," "dumped," "put on the street," "fired," "laid off": regardless of the terminology or circumstance, the result is the same: Everyone here is unemployed. Waiting in line for hours, wearing the scarlet U, fuels the emerging sparks of anger toward the company that left you in such a situation. This is only the beginning.

As humiliating and bleak as the application process may be, unemployment insurance benefits do provide some relief and ensure the probability of food on the table. The concept of unemployment assistance arose out of the Great Depression in an effort to assist employees on a short-term basis (currently, twenty-six weeks) or until other employment was secured. Some states have extensions for another twelve weeks if joblessness is severe.

Within the ranks of those who are still employed, it is common to hear such proclamations as, "If they let me go, no sweat; I'll just collect my unemployment, sit back, and enjoy the good life." Well, don't join the yacht club just yet.

The rules governing the administration of unemployment vary from state to state, but most require that you lost your job through no fault of your own in order to qualify for benefits. These plans are designed to replace one-half of the lost salary, provided it doesn't exceed some rather meager limits. The maximum for those who qualify is usually below the minimum wage level, which is also considered taxable income by the IRS. Those who are living on unemployment, provided there is no other source of income for the family, are at or below the poverty level as established by the U.S. government. To continue receiving these benefits, most states require that recipients attend a quota of documented job interviews.

Experts have written not a few books on the emotional aspects of job loss and job search strategies. Most draw a parallel of job loss to the grieving process following the death of someone close and a mourning period for healthy recovery. To fail to acknowledge these feelings and work through the grieving process leads to frustration and increased stress.

Life as Usual

Although the emotional impact can be devastating, my advice to newly laid-off employees is to keep to much the same schedule as when employed. Continuing to start the day off in much the same way as before gives a sense of purpose in life. It is important to stay physically and mentally active during this time. Much like climbing back on the proverbial horse after being thrown, the sooner the energy is channeled to structured job-seeking activities, the better. Allow yourself the luxury of grieving for a time, but don't give in to the urge to give up on trying to move forward.

Facing the Family

At a time when family support is of critical importance, the bonds may stretch to the limit as the family scrambles to deal with the crisis. Financial stresses and disagreements are the leading causes of marital discord and, ultimately, divorce, so it is no surprise that research shows couples are far more likely to be divorced after the intrusion of a layoff into the marriage. Even the strongest marriages are tested. As one partner swings between anger and depression in dealing with the severe blow to the self-esteem, the other carries on the activities of daily living.

The same tide of a layoff that pummels the employee also washes over the entire family unit. If the laid-off employee is the primary breadwinner, the family may have to switch roles for a time.

Children are not immune to the effects of a layoff. Their feeling of security and well-being will likely be shaken. Children, particularly young children, look to their parents as very powerful figures. When something negative happens to either parent, who seems to have no control over it, it can be as frightening to the child as if his or her own safety is at risk. Trying to hide the situation from the kids is a noble gesture but one likely to fail. A more logical approach is to explain, according to their level of understanding, the changes that have come about. By taking an honest and straightforward approach, children are more likely to cooperate with any financial sacrifices that they may need to make.

Facing the Finances

Being laid off means the loss of money. The loss of money threatens basic survival, and that fear clouds everything. Visions of the cardboard boxes that serve as shelter for the homeless and the malnourished children in the world mercilessly torment the dreams of the newly unemployed. The loss of income brings with it a perceived loss of power and control over life. Here are some ways to cope with the finances:

▪ *Examine every expense in the household budget,* no matter how small or insignificant it may seem. Can you live without it for a time? Some quiet money nibblers are cable or pay TV, fitness club memberships, extra telephone features, fast foods, and computer on-line services. Even the most conservative budgets can usually shave off some extra here and there.

▪ *Protect your credit history.* Most creditors agree that the most effective way to preserve a good credit history in the case of a financial downturn is to take an active stance. Creditors are far more likely to play hardball if they don't hear from you. Many are understanding and are willing to extend some leniency in the case of hardship. Contact creditors in writing before they send late-payment notices, when they may be less willing to negotiate terms. Explain your situation and request a month or two of reduced payments.

Even if you emerge with a damaged credit rating, it can be repaired. A letter to the credit bureau explaining the situation, with the request that it be included in your file, may be of help later. Remember that the most important aspect here is to show a willingness to work with the creditors and to work at repairing any marred credit after you secure employment. Creditors are usually more concerned about a pattern of poor risk, not a one-time slump in the financial picture.

▪ *Talk to the utility companies and find out if they have a payment-averaging program over the course of the year.* Averaging gives a concrete figure to budget every month and avoids seasonal highs and lows. Most of these companies will not disconnect basic service as long as they receive even a partial payment every month.

▪ *What about that second car?* Is it absolutely necessary? Could it be garaged for a temporary time or even sold? Car payments, maintenance, and insurance drain large amounts of cash.

▪ *Don't pay anything that doesn't have to be paid.* This will help preserve the cash on hand to stretch over several months if necessary.

▪ *Should you consider bankruptcy,* an increasingly popular way to deal with acute financial pressures? (In a one-year period, from July 1, 1990, to June 30, 1991, bankruptcies increased nationally at the alarming rate of 21.4 percent.) This process holds the creditors at bay and may protect the individual's home. Be aware that while bankruptcy does offer some temporary relief from the pressure, it will also result in some long-lasting credit damage. Future creditors may be reluctant to lend to an individual with a history of bankruptcy long after the financial picture has changed.

Insurance Woes

A laid-off employee is guaranteed the right to continue the group health insurance for up to 18 months. This right is protected under the 1985 federal Consolidated Omnibus Budget Reconciliation Act (COBRA). However, the ex-employee usually has to pay the full premium for this coverage, unless that point has been negotiated in the severance agreement, and premiums can run as high as $600 or more each month for a family. (Clearly this is a valuable asset to negotiate into the severance agreement.)

You have the option to discontinue this coverage at any time, but the advice is usually to accept the coverage and pay the premium until further employment or more affordable insurance is found. Some insurance providers offer temporary catastrophic coverage for those who find themselves suddenly without any health insurance. This kind of plan, however, may require several months' premiums to be paid in advance, and they are often nonrefundable.

Considering that many illnesses are stress related, this is not a good time to go without health insurance coverage.

To Sue or Not to Sue

As you fume over these jobless indignities, you might wonder whether to consult with an attorney about bringing some action against your former employer, but this is not an easy path to follow. Chances are very good that the layoff decision and process were reviewed by the company's legal staff to ensure that no loopholes existed. A good attorney, however, can be very helpful in negotiating a fair severance package with severance pay, prolonged insurance benefits, and favorable references for future use in job seeking. Be aware that once an attorney is involved, the process may slow down and postpone or even reduce the receipt of the initial benefits.

Increasingly companies are having employees sign away the right to sue for civil rights violations and agree, instead, to binding arbitration in the case of a dispute. In fact, some companies have made forfeiting the right to sue a requirement for employment, promotion, or some benefits such as stock options. So before you hire an attorney, find out what you may have signed away in better times.

If you still want to consult an attorney, find one who is reputable and experienced. Most attorneys do not charge for an initial consultation to discuss the case; this meeting should identify what you might gain by pursuing action against the ex-employer. Talking to people who have had cases in similar situations may also be helpful. If you suspect discrimination or wrongful discharge, it is vital that you consult an attorney.

The Job Search

Regardless of the circumstances surrounding the layoff, one of your most crucial tasks is to review and update your resumé. It may be well worth seeking help from a professional, especially if your resumé is poorly prepared. The old adage "First impressions make lasting impressions" is certainly true here. An outdated resumé that is filled with typos or one that looks like a poor photocopy screams of some very negative traits to the prospective employer.

To bolster the bruised self-esteem that comes with a layoff, you may be tempted to include every detail of your professional life in the resumé. However, depending on the type of job you seek, less may be more. Consider preparing several versions of a resumé slanted to different types of employment, with emphasis and more detail on the related qualifications. Of course, never lie or purposely omit relevant information. "Dumbing down" a resumé to go after a job is not a good practice, either. Hiring executives are wary of these tactics and will reject an otherwise qualified employee based on the perception of untrustworthiness. Polled executives estimate that one-third of all resumés contain such blunders.

Armed with your revised resumé, embark on your journey. Most likely it will be long and rough. Few people are equipped to handle comfortably the rejections that inevitably come with a layoff and resulting job search. "Overqualified," "underqualified," and "no availability" are words that become arrows. With every rejection comes a new wave of anger toward the former employer coupled with further erosion of an already fragile self-esteem. Forced out of the comfortable haven that has been a sec-

ond home for many years, you are forced into a new and sometimes cutthroat environment that permeates a job search. You
may be tempted to snatch the first offer of employment that
comes along to avoid complete annihilation. This, however, may
be a disastrous choice that only accelerates your career's downward spiral.

Out of the Loop

Dealing with being laid off is no picnic. Little things become big
things. The first time your friends want you to go to lunch or a
movie or even a weekend trip, the stake sinks a little deeper.
Knowing that you must squeeze the life out of every penny, you
can't afford to spend the money. Besides, the guilt that you feel
if you do decide to throw caution to the winds can ruin the
occasion.

Old friends back at work may not feel comfortable contact-
ing you. After all, what is there to talk about? "Why are you still
there and I'm not?" Conversation is uncomfortable at best and
leaves fresh wounds at worst. Your old boss may even discourage such contacts and maintain an air of secrecy that implies a
sinister reason for your firing.

Personal friends may seem distant. Imagine the first church
or synagogue service you attend after the layoff. Nothing has
outwardly changed, and you maintain your usual, friendly de-
meanor. "See me. I'm fine. Really." As you stand amid all the
buzz of friendly conversation, you become acutely aware of how
much of life's conversation is centered around business. One of
the more devastating moments comes when you walk up to a
group sharing the week's war stories from work, and everyone
falls silent. They have heard the news. Every fiber in you wants
to scream to the world that you are still a person, a person who
has something to offer in this world, that you did nothing to
deserve the ax—but the words remain unsaid and the half-smile
remains. You're not sure whether it is flattery or humility you
feel when they ask to take you to lunch.

Recovery from the scourge of layoff is possible. It is painful
and tedious and requires determination, persistence, and plan-

ning. If anything good can be said about a layoff it is that it offers the opportunity to make some inward and outward changes that can greatly improve the quality of your life. Whether you choose reemployment or self-employment, life after a layoff can be better than what it was before.

John's Story

John, a good friend of mine, was in his late thirties and a manager for an international corporation. Friendly by nature, he had everything going for him: a good salary, a secure job, a good marriage, and two beautiful children. Everything in his life was enviable and secure, he thought, until the day that he collapsed with a heart attack. He recovered from this devastating experience and returned to his job fresh out of rehabilitation and stress management classes, and with a new enthusiasm for life.

But even as he lay in a hospital bed, the corporate decision makers were plotting his removal from the company. Shortly after he returned to work, the layoff hatchet severed John's relationship with the company.

John was devastated. He and his wife scrutinized every conceivable option to reestablish an income. Realizing their love of dogs might hold potential for income, John and his wife opened a dog grooming and boarding service and began raising their own show dogs. Now they have a thriving pet store and grooming parlor.

More than ten years have passed since his layoff, but John and his wife acutely remember the sting. Still, their story offers hope and encouragement to those who find themselves in a similar predicament. Did they struggle? You had better believe it. There were times that they didn't know where the next meal was coming from or how to buy the children a warm coat, but they persevered and pulled together to make it through.

John's success may not be typical of the unemployed. He will tell you that his road to recovery has not been smooth. In fact, he may even discourage you from following in his footsteps. Though he does not regret the path he chose, he knows that several years of his life would have been more enjoyable if he had been given time and notice to make such a dramatic change in his career. Had he been able to make a gentle transition from employee to small business owner, he could have minimized the hardship and risk he and his family have endured.

A layoff forces some difficult choices. Some people will have more flexibility than others in how they choose. Whatever path is taken, it is important to develop a structured plan and put the plan into action as soon as possible. Survival requires one to create the future while healing the past—a combination that is neither easy nor noble. It is simply survival.

10

The Cruelest Cut: Laying Off Older Workers

If I were going to weep for anybody today, I would weep for the middle-level people. If an employer has a choice of someone three years out of business school or someone age 50, which will they select? I'm afraid the job goes to the younger person.

Irving S. Shapiro,
Chairman and CEO, du Pont

The scene is at once grandiose and tragic. Gliding across the stage of *Sunset Boulevard* is the aging actress Norma Desmond, whose classic beauty and melodramatic stances are no longer needed by a Hollywood that has no appetite for silent movies or older actresses. In this scene, Norma has arrived on the sound stage of a "talking" movie mistakenly thinking that director Cecil B. DeMille had summoned her back to work. Suddenly one of the lighting crewmen recognizes the now forgotten star who has just entered the room, and he swings the spotlight on to her. She lifts her head to the cameras and sings haunting lyrics about a career that has been cut mercilessly short.

Norma Desmond isn't alone in feeling discarded. Those words ring with meaning today for many middle-aged workers who have been laid off or coerced into early retirement. Despite the desire to keep working, these workers are told their skills are obsolete and their jobs have disappeared. They find themselves without work, without income, and without the retirement they had worked hard to achieve. At a time in their lives when they hoped to enjoy the reward of their labors, they find themselves scouring the want ads and standing in line at the unemployment office. Layoffs hit older workers harder than any other group in society.

Ironically, workers over age 40 come from a generation with the strongest loyalty to the company and the healthiest work ethic of any other in this century. For the most part, they have willingly given their requisite pound of flesh. They have worked uncountable 60- and 70-hour weeks, sacrificed time with their families, arranged weddings and other significant life events around their work schedule, moved to parts unknown at the bidding of the company, and gone to night school to get that stylish M.B.A. And why did they do this? Because of some morally driven need to sacrifice themselves for the sake of the company? Hardly. They did it under the mistaken promise that it would secure their future.

The Employer-Employee Contract

Since the early part of this century, workers have enjoyed a strong social contract with their employers. It was a demanding agreement, but it worked well for both the company and the employee. The terms of that contract went something like this:

> The worker agrees to give his time, energy, and knowledge to the company in the performance of the job that is given him. He agrees to show up at the appointed time (or earlier if necessary) dressed in the prescribed uniform, alert, and ready to work. The worker is expected to comply with all requests presented him by the company. These requests may include, but are not limited to, such things as traveling overnight for as long as is needed, working late into the evening, moving one's household and family to a new job site, and taking the occasional job that is not of interest but for the good of the company. Most important, the worker is expected to meet and exceed

performance standards of whatever job he is given to perform.

In exchange, the company agrees to provide the worker with ongoing employment. If the worker complies with all requests and performs in accordance with performance standards, he can expect occasional increases in salary and promotions into jobs of increasing responsibility. The company agrees to provide health care and various other insurances for the worker and his family. Finally, after a career of service to the company, the company will provide the worker with a pension that will enable the worker to retire from full-time employment.

This contract is the reason older workers have given so much to their jobs. This trade-off benefited both the worker and the company: The employee agreed to work hard and make whatever sacrifices were required, and the company agreed to provide the worker with security—ongoing employment, health care, salary, and retirement.

Now, after several very difficult recessions, companies have found this agreement to be too expensive. Promises of continuous employment create an ongoing liability for the company that prefers to staff up during good times and slim down during the bad. Health care has become increasingly costly, causing employers to cut those benefits back or drop them altogether. Some companies, like TWA, have even raided pension funds, jeopardizing the retirement benefits of workers, past and present.

To get out of this costly obligation, many companies are using the tactic of claiming that there never was a so-called social contract. Instead, they paint the picture that for years they mistakenly fed the growing sense of entitlement among the workforce but never committed to provide these benefits. They were simply extras that were given to the workforce when times were better, and now regrettably, workers have come to expect them.

What has really happened is that most companies have been silently rewriting the contract. According to these new terms, today's workers have a right to expect payment for work being currently performed and nothing more—no expectations of on-going employment, future promotions, or pay increases. The doctrine of employment-at-will (although rejected by the courts) is a favorite among most companies: The company can choose to hire or fire an employee at will, for any reason. It absolves the company of any ongoing commitment to the employee beyond payment for services rendered.

Imagine the shock of older workers who have been toiling away for some thirty years under the impression of the old con-tract when the layoff ax falls. It is hard for them to believe their misfortune when junior staffers hand them a severance agree-ment and disavow any knowledge of the terms of the unwritten contract. The business has moved on, and there is no place in its future for them, they are told.

The impact of a layoff on older workers is profound. Be-cause so many of them have trusted the company to provide for them as they approach retirement, they are unprepared for the psychological and financial consequences of a layoff. Many have spent a career working for a single company. They are en-trenched in the ways and technologies of their company—something that is not easily transferred or even desired by a new employer. Chances are that they have been highly paid by a compensation system that is designed to reward longevity and loyalty to the company. If they are lucky enough to land a new job, more often than not they find themselves underemployed, underpaid, and frustrated by the ways of the new company.

As a result, the majority of those older workers who are laid off retreat into early retirement. They scale back their standard of living and expectations for the future. Wearied by the pros-pect of starting over again, they elect to withdraw from the world of employment and pursue whatever interests and hob-bies they might now afford.

Purging the Payroll

Jonathan Kellet's Story

Jonathan Kellet knew what he wanted. He had had one girl-friend, Joan, and he married her for life. He went to the home-town college and got the business degree he signed up for the first day of his freshman year. After graduation, he joined the home office of an insurance company headquartered in his native Nebraska. For thirty-two years he gratefully climbed that same corporate ladder.

At age 54 and after thirty-two years with the company, Jonathan had become sales director, one of the highest positions in the company. During his tenure, Jonathan had hired many sales managers and promoted the careers of countless promising managers, including the meteoric career of the current CEO. Jonathan was a fixture around his company and knew virtually every aspect of the business.

Jonathan enjoyed the rewards that come from thirty years of raises and promotions. He had earned passage to the executive wing and the paycheck that comes with it. Among the highest-paid employees, he was also one of the oldest, so it wasn't surprising when Jonathan learned he was being promoted to regional vice president. Five new regional VP positions were being created, and he and four of his colleagues of similar age and salary were being promoted into these positions. Jonathan was given the Southwest region based out of Phoenix. After much deliberation, he decided to move from the state of his birth for the first time in his life. He and Joan sold the family home, said good-bye to lifelong friends, and let the company move them to Phoenix.

Two years later, after setting up the new regional office, Jonathan and the other regional VPs were summoned to corporate headquarters in Omaha. There had been a change in the way their new jobs would be structured. Their primary task would now be recruitment of new sales managers, and they would have a quota of new recruits to hire per quarter. All hiring decisions, of course, would be made pending headquarters approval. Before returning to their regions, each VP was asked to sign a statement agreeing to the quota.

A year after that meeting, not one of the regional VPs had met his quota. Not that they hadn't tried, but headquarters refused to approve all but the most stellar of recruits they presented, giving little reason for those rejected. As a result of what the company deemed poor performance, each of the regional

VPs, including Jonathan, was called in and pressured to take early retirement or a demotion back at the home office. All but one retired, and he was later fired. Afterward, the company decided not to rehire for the regional positions.

The company had found a convenient way to purge its payroll of some of the high rollers. No doubt these older gentlemen were seen by their younger counterparts as kindly father figures, now somewhat obsolete. They were gently moved away from the visibility of the corporate headquarters and cleanly dumped. By creating the illusion of poor performance by the signed agreements and bogus quotas, they strongly discouraged any of the terminated from risking their life savings in a lawsuit. Who wouldn't accept the partial payment of early retirement rather than risk everything on a lawsuit they might not win?

How Big Is the Problem?

Jonathan's situation is by no means unique. With downsizing efforts admittedly aimed at middle management (meaning workers over age 40), large numbers of older, mid-career workers have unexpectedly found themselves unemployed. The actual number is hard to pin down; many of these workers "voluntarily" resign or take early retirement and are not counted in the typical layoff numbers.

One snapshot of how many older workers have been affected comes from a nonscientific survey conducted by the American Association for Retired Persons (AARP). Of the 10,000 respondents, all over the age of 45, two-thirds reported that they had left their jobs under duress. By a two-to-one margin they believed their dismissals violated the Age Discrimination in Employment Act (ADEA). Of those who were able to find other employment, four out of five said that the new job paid less than their previous one.

The figures from any one layoff often do not show a disproportionate number of older workers being laid off. Because of the potential for costly litigation under the ADEA, companies carefully monitor who is technically classified as a layoff victim. When Kmart laid off 900 workers two weeks before Christmas 1994 at its Troy, Michigan, headquarters, managers circulated spreadsheets showing the layoffs by birthdates in an effort to prove that older workers were not disproportionally affected.

Instead, the higher-paid older workers are often pushed out using the more coercive, one-on-one techniques discussed earlier in this book. Rather than move far away from family and lifelong friends or take a position beneath their level of achievement, these workers opt to take a severance package and leave the company. With the payout often comes a signed agreement not to disclose the terms of the package, not to speak disparagingly about the company, and not to bring suit against the company. With no other viable options, they take the money, sign the agreement, and return home to nurse their wounds and allow the anger to subside.

Finding a new job is particularly difficult for workers over age 55. Scott Bass, a gerontologist at the University of Massachusetts, found that it takes these workers twice as long to find employment as it does for the rest of the population seeking work. When work is found, it almost always offers less money and challenge than the previous career-track position. The prospects are so limited that many of these workers stop looking and become part of the "discouraged workers" category. Since federal unemployment figures count only those who are unemployed and looking for work, these "discouraged workers" drop out of the statistical picture. In one year, the federal government estimated this group of older, discouraged workers to be 168,000. Many in the gerontology field, including former federal gerontologist W. Ray Smith, consider the actual number to be much higher.

One reason these older, discarded employees have trouble finding work lies in the very programs designed to enhance retirement: defined pension plans. Under these traditional retirement programs, newly hired older workers require a much greater contribution to the pension plan than younger workers. When you couple that considerable expense with the progressive salary increases inherent in the more senior resumé, you find that older workers are far more expensive than their younger counterparts. Given a choice, most companies opt for the younger, "bargain basement" employee.

Suing for Age Discrimination

But wait a minute! If older workers are being discriminated against, don't they have some recourse through the courts? They do, but it is difficult for most. Picture yourself having spent twenty, thirty, maybe even forty years of your life working for a company. You have spent a lifetime making friends out of co-workers who worked shoulder to shoulder with you to bring the company success. You believed in the company, its values and its leadership. Now, in a few days' time, you must forget all of that history and make an enemy out of the organization to which you were once devoted. In some ways, filing a lawsuit invalidates everything you stood for throughout your career. It is a really tough psychological line to cross, and not many laid-off workers, even out of their anger and pain, are willing to do it.

Of those who do, the process grinds very slowly, and proving the discrimination can be a nightmare. Every performance review, interoffice memo, and discussion with the supervisor is dragged into the courtroom in an effort to show that the firing was justified. Technically sophisticated statistical models are presented in an attempt to show that older workers were not adversely affected by the layoff. In short, proving age discrimination can turn out to be very upsetting and difficult. And after all this, you could still lose and walk away with nothing.

Nevertheless, complaints of age discrimination are on the rise. In Massachusetts, age discrimination complaints have more than doubled in the past ten years. Nationally, these complaints are on the rise and account for roughly 25 percent of all cases filed at the Equal Employment Opportunity Commission. Of these, state and national agencies will turn out only about 14 percent of the cases successfully for the complaint, primarily because they could not come up with the required evidence.

Age discrimination is against the law. Unfortunately, many labor attorneys consider it a well-formulated law with poor enforcement. According to Martin Sicker, director of AARP's workforce programs, "If a company does it cleverly, it can discriminate with impunity."

The Move Toward a Younger Workforce

One of the underlying motivations for laying off older workers comes from a strongly held belief about youth. Youth is associated with energy, alertness, creativity, health, and ambition in the minds of many. Corporate managers take these beliefs and infuse them into hiring and firing practices, hoping to energize their business. One of the best examples of this in practice comes from the Gap headquarters in San Francisco. The mean age of employees of this highly successful retail giant couldn't be more than about 26 or 27 years old. One former human resources manager from the Gap told me that the organization specifically targets hiring toward candidates in their early twenties. Management believes that younger employees have more "hip" ideas and that older workers are less willing to drive themselves so hard. The company has long engaged in the practice of hiring young, eager employees and working them nonstop until they burn out a few years later.

Another company known for its younger-than-average employees is Lotus Development Corporation. In 1994, Lotus was sued by Carol Moskowitz, who was laid off after she turned 50. During the trial, a Lotus human resources manager testified that she had circled Moskowitz's age on a list of employees being considered for the layoff but did not use that information in Moskowitz's firing. Lotus defended its youthful employee base by saying that only young people wanted to work for the company. The court, however, didn't buy it and awarded Moskowitz $275,000.

Could it be that companies like the Gap and Lotus are justified in seeking a younger workforce? After all, the Gap does market to young, trendy shoppers, and Lotus is designing software for those younger computer jockeys who journey through cyberspace. But a hard look at the evidence shows no relationship between the age of a company's workforce and its creativity or technical sophistication. In the case of the Gap, the vast majority of fashion designers who are popular among young shoppers are over age 40. Furthermore, any visit to a Gap store shows plenty of shoppers beyond thirty-something. As for Lotus, the notion that only young people are using personal computers is false. CompUSA, the national computer store, estimates that half of all systems it sells through its retail stores are to customers over 40 years old who intend to use the computer for home office applications. Computers are by no means the sole property of the younger generations. The idea that fashion retailing, computer usage, or any other type of work is best done by younger workers is nothing more than erroneous, stereotypic thinking.

Americans aren't the only ones glorifying youth in the workplace, either. In October 1994, Toyota Motor Corporation announced that it wanted a more youthful look. To achieve this corporate facelift, Toyota set a rule that deputy general managers could be no older than 53 and section chiefs no older than 50. Managers who reached these age limits were reassigned to "special projects." A Toyota spokesperson said this move was taken to rejuvenate management's ranks.

Increasingly senior managements view older workers as expensive, somewhat obsolete, and resistant to change. Young workers have a more current education and are seen as being more flexible and willing to change. Moreover, they can be hired for much less than their more senior counterparts, they don't care about expensive retirement benefits, and they are less likely to become a drain on the company health plan. Economically, youth makes a better deal. Consequently, financial analysts' and senior executives' talk about cutting from the bloated, sluggish middle ranks is code for dumping older and more expensive employees.

The Pension Fund Raid

The desire for a younger workforce isn't the only motivation to lay off older workers. A covert force at work is compelling organizations to cut workers from the payroll before they become eligible for full retirement benefits. It is called the underfunding of pension funds, and it is a problem that has risen to crisis proportions in the United States.

During the 1980s and early 1990s, nearly 2,000 corporations dipped into pension funds for at least $1 million each, bringing the total take from the funds set aside for the retirement of older workers to just over $21 billion. And where did all this money go? The biggest chunk went to finance leveraged buyouts and corporate mergers. The rest went directly into the company's cash account and eventually ended up in the pockets of aggressive corporate raiders who are often the primary shareholders. One corporate raider, Victor Posner, has drained the pension funds of eight companies he acquired over the past ten years to the tune of $65.2 million.

The list of companies with underfunded pensions is staggering. Among the top fifty companies according to the Pension Benefit Guaranty Corporation (the quasi-government organization that insures pension funds) are Chrysler Corporation with a $2.6 billion deficit and Boise Cascade at $32 million in the red. The list of those companies with underfunded pensions grows longer each year, prompting James B. Lockhart III, executive director of Pension Benefit Guaranty Corporation, to warn that there is "at least $40 billion of unfunded liabilities in the defined pensions system."

So how does all of this high finance affect the layoff of older workers? It provides direct financial incentive to keep the pension roster to a minimum. As long as fewer retirees are receiving payments, the underfunding of the pension fund may never become a serious problem. In other words, if fewer employees retire at full retirement benefits, there may turn out to be enough money to go around after all. By laying off workers before they are vested in the pension plan and forcing others to retire early with a greatly reduced pension, the demand on the shrinking pension funds diminishes greatly. Some companies have even gone a step further by constantly churning their workforce at all ages to ensure that very few employees survive a career-long obstacle course of layoffs until retirement.

The Wisdom of Age

Not everything that is being touted about younger employees is truth. In fact, much of it has little basis in fact. True, younger workers do cost less in terms of salary, health benefits, and retirement pensions. But it isn't true that they are more motivated or creative workers. The inexperience of their youth often creates enormous inefficiencies, and they require much more training than do more experienced workers. Younger employees are much more likely to jump from job to job, costing the company plenty in lost productivity and hiring costs. Considering that many companies estimate that an employee isn't profitable until he or she has been six months on the job, this hidden cost of job jumping quickly eats into any salary savings.

Ironically, the senior managers who are pushing the trend toward youth are anything but young themselves. And it isn't by chance that executive boardrooms sport plenty of gray hair. Age brings with it a tempered wisdom and leadership talents. Experience alone seems to be the best teacher of how to lead people. Without the benefit of age, very few are able to handle the demands of a senior executive position. Unfortunately, this truism of the upper ranks isn't applied to the middle or lower management tiers.

There is no substitute for the learning that comes with experience. A great example comes from the story told around Hewlett-Packard of a general manager who made a multimillion-dollar business error. When the mistake came to the attention of company owner David Packard, he called the general manager in for what everyone assumed would be his last conference with the president. Much to everyone's surprise, the fellow emerged from the meeting unscathed and returned to his position as general manager. When asked why he didn't fire him, David Packard is said to have replied, "Why should I fire him? I just paid several million dollars for him to learn a difficult lesson." Regretfully, this truth that older workers have the wisdom of trial and error on their side is increasingly lost in the rush toward a younger workforce.

Layoffs have hit older workers hard. Despite decades of commitment and hard work, these corporate veterans are finding that history is meaningless to companies determined to raise *this* quarter's earnings. Many senior managers feel no obligation to the sacrifices these workers may have made in the past. As the corporate periscope narrows on profit, there is no room for those older workers, who are incorrectly believed to be less profitable and a drag on the organization.

11

Personal Layoff Protection

The personal cost of being laid off can be devastating for the unprepared. When the steady cycle of paychecks comes to a slamming halt, a person's financial situation can go from good to disastrous in less than 24 hours. Here's what happened to one traveling manager after being laid off:

I think it was Saturday morning. It's hard to say, because every day felt like Saturday morning after I was laid off—not the picnic-in-the-park kind of Saturday but the kind of ambivalent, not-really-sure-what-to-do kind of Saturday. It was as if I knew there was something I should be doing, but, for the life of me, I couldn't remember what it was. The one time anchor I had left after my boss permanently cleared my calendar was the daily "power" meeting I had at 11 A.M. It was an important meeting—the one thing that forced me out of my robe and slippers and into something more presentable. Every day Sam and I met at the foot of my driveway. Every day he would deliver my mail.

The one day I remember well was several weeks after my desk was "relocated" from the office to the guest bedroom. On this day, an envelope arrived from the company I used to work for. When I saw the logo emblazoned on the envelope peeking from behind the stack of soon-to-be-past-due bills, my heart raced and my hands trembled. Could it be that they have finally come to their senses and realized they can't possibly run that office without me? Would it be a letter of apology and an invitation to return? Probably not. But maybe they did decide to rethink that tightfisted severance policy. That's it—it would be a check to supplement that dwindling handout they gave me as they swept me out the back door.

When I opened the envelope and read the letter, my nervous anticipation turned to angry disbelief. They regretted to inform me that due to my recent "change of employment status," the entire balance of the car they financed for me was now due. It was thousands of dollars—thousands of dollars I didn't have. Wasn't it enough that they took away my paycheck? Now they wanted payment in full for a used company car I purchased that had long passed its prime. Furious, I dug through my files searching for the finance contract. To my horror, there it was in the fine print: the entire balance was due upon termination.

Protecting against a layoff before it happens is something that few think to do but many wish they had. An unexpected layoff can ravage your finances and shake your confidence in ways that can take years from which to recover. Most of us take a this-can't-happen-to-me approach to layoffs, so we aren't prepared when it does happen. We run our careers and finances as if my job is really *my* job. In the age of layoffs, nobody owns their job. Layoffs happen to the best of employees, and chances are it will eventually happen to you.

By the way, if you are lulled into thinking that because you have the inside track on layoffs at your company you won't be axed, think again. Middle managers and Human Resources, the two groups most in the know and most involved in planning a layoff, are also the most commonly targeted groups. Many companies have shown little mercy to those who have helped wield the ax. Repeatedly companies have not hesitated to lay off those who helped to lay off others.

Whatever your situation is, you can reduce your chances of being laid off and prepare yourself in the eventuality that you are. Aside from the usual "keep your head down and nose clean" advice, there are specific actions you can take that will reduce your chances of becoming the next corporate cost-cutter target. But before we look at those, take a minute and assess your own susceptibility to a layoff.

An Ounce of Prevention

How many of these statements are true for you?

☐ You have taken a "promote me or lose me" stance, and no one cares.

☐ Your pay raises have been slim to none over the past years.

☐ Your boss asks you, "What kind of future do you see for yourself here?"

☐ The market demand for your company's product or services is diminishing.

☐ A corporate raider is bidding for your company.

☐ You are the highest-paid person in your department, and business is declining.

☐ Your performance review is more than three months past due.

☐ You haven't received a bonus in the past couple of years.

☐ Your boss is slowly taking away your job responsibilities.

☐ Key executives are regularly canceling meetings you have scheduled.

If you find yourself answering yes to one or more of these statements, you may be in imminent danger of being laid off. It is a sign that you need to take some action to protect your job. Here are a few steps you might consider:

* *Cross-train.* The most proactive action you can take to protect yourself against a layoff is to cross-train rigorously on skills outside your traditional job description. Think of it as job insurance. Employees who upgrade their skills by learning new tasks on the job or by taking classes throughout their careers are more valuable to their employers. If your current duties are slated to be dropped, you have another cadre of skills you can

employ on another job that is staying or will be created as a result of the layoff. During times of a layoff, employers value flexibility and the ability to change far more than they value finely tuned expertise.

Cross-training means keeping up with rapidly changing work methods, technologies, and issues that affect your industry. One of the quickest ways to become a layoff victim is to tell your boss, "That's not how we've always done it," or, "I only do it this way." Demonstrating your diversity of skills and knowledge of new technology will ensure the company that you will continue to provide a useful service even if your job changes or is eliminated.

» *Don't play politics.* Playing the political field in your favor can do wonders for your career in better times, but it isn't a good idea when times are less favorable. Restructurings shift the balance of corporate power, and the executive who is in today may be on the outs tomorrow, and following right behind him or her will be all of those who were closely aligned. Perhaps it isn't right or even fair, but it is the way the game is played when someone has to be let go. Keeping a low political profile and maintaining good relations across the board is a good strategy for protection.

» *Mind your corporate manners.* Some of the more common-sense aspects of prevention fall into the category of good corporate etiquette:

» Exercise professional office behavior and know what to avoid.
» Reserve your complaints for the right time and place.
» Avoid whining and complaining about your job or the company while at work.
» Don't associate closely with those who might be seen as troublemakers or chronic complainers.
» Keep a close watch on your sick time. Fight the temptation to use it, except, of course, when you are really sick.
» Avoid talking about personal difficulties at work. Marital and personal financial problems are better discussed with true friends rather than the company lunchroom gossips.

▪ Always avoid emotional outbursts at work. Memories of temper tantrums and hysterical crying linger in the boss's mind long after the last tear has dried. All too often those who freely display their hearts are branded as irrational and undependable.

▪ *Manage your career.* Don't wait for someone else to push you forward; take the initiative to set your own goals for advancement. Look around, and find out what promotions you might be ready to take. Let the powers that be know you are interested and eager to advance. Don't just limit yourself to inside the company either. Keep an updated resumé handy, and always return a headhunter's call. You can always turn an offer down, but you can't accept an offer that isn't there.

Protection Against Future Shock

Sometimes there is little you can do to prevent the inevitable layoff, but even in this situation, you aren't completely helpless. Here are a few suggestions about what you can do right now that will minimize the damage of layoff should it happen to you:

▪ *Always practice reverse performance management.* Make sure your performance reviews are up to date. If they are not, be insistent about a timely, written review. Then ensure that every rating in the review is documented with valid examples of your performance (this is always a good idea, even if a layoff isn't lurking). If you notice a decrease in rating from a previous review, question the change carefully. Let your boss know that you are aware of the change and you want to know exactly what has caused it. Between reviews, tactfully keep your boss informed about all of your accomplishments on a regular basis. Make sure he or she knows the value of your contribution to the company. Finally, keep a work journal. Every day, or at least weekly, make notes in your calendar about what you did: discussions you had with your boss, customers or coworkers you worked with, and so forth. Often laid-off employees recognize the manipulative, termination-oriented actions after it is too late.

By documenting every day, you are stashing away bargaining chips that could be handy in a negotiation with your former employer.

□ *Put your payroll deductions in an easily liquidated savings plan.* Losing a paycheck can be financially devastating. Without a paycheck, income comes to a sudden halt, but the bills do not. One of the most important ways to protect yourself is to take a close look at your payroll deduction savings plans. Are all of your savings in a 401K, Individual Retirement Account (IRA), or some other retirement account? Although these accounts are excellent and fairly painless savings methods, they do not offer ready cash when a crisis occurs, and the penalty for withdrawal prior to retirement age is significant. There is also a small window of time following termination in which changes can be made to these accounts. In the aftermath of an unexpected layoff, that window may close before you are able to review the options and make a wise decision.

Make sure a sizable portion of your savings goes to a cash account that can be liquidated on demand and with little penalty in the event you need to supplement your income while you look for work. Even if you have to reduce your contributions to a 401K or retirement account to establish liquid savings, it is well worth it. Another smart strategy is to try to reduce your overall debt and buy layoff insurance for loans when you can.

□ *Examine your retirement account, especially a 401K plan.* Since the money in 401K accounts is invested in stock and, according to one survey, the majority of companies invest 36 to 49 percent of 401K money in their own stock, there is great potential for loss during a layoff. Imagine that two decades ago you signed up to buy shares in your company through a stock purchase account. In the 1980s, you rolled it over to a 401K plan and acquired even more company stock. Now, twenty years later, you discover that you have been laid off and must sell the stock in your account. When you check the newspaper, the stock is trading at $50—right where it was when you started, and far below the price you paid for many of the shares when the stock was at a high of $170. You and all of your former coworkers lost $2.5 billion in less than two years between 1989 and 1991. What company's stock would take employees for such a wild ride? The quintessential blue-chip company: International Business Machines.

What happened at IBM is a lesson to all who want to protect their retirement against a layoff. If the company is doing poorly and responds by laying off employees, as did IBM, the newly laid-off employees can realize huge losses because they are required to cash in their stock when the company is doing badly. Most financial planners suggest employees over 40 years of age should invest no more than 10 percent of retirement funds in company stock. Anything more is risky business.

On the subject of retirement accounts, there is one point of particular interest to the newly laid off. If your IRA was set up by your employer, you may be given the option of allowing the employer to hold the account until you are 65, thus avoiding the 10 percent penalty for early withdrawal. If not, your employer should withhold 20 percent for income taxes, leaving only the 10 percent penalty to be paid by you. In any event, it is a much safer option to set up your own IRA account. Should you be laid off, you will not be forced to withdraw the money and can avoid the early withdrawal penalty.

- *Network, network, network.* Since getting the income flowing again is a primary concern, take steps before you are laid off that will hasten your job search should you become unemployed. As one ex-school-teacher-turned-outplacement-counselor sang to a group of incredulous layoff victims, "A networking we go!" The truth remains that networking is the most valuable way you can jump-start your stalled career, and it is most valuable and effective *before* you are laid off.

Two avenues for career networking are professional organizations and outside consultants. Although professional organizations almost always meet in a cheap hotel that serves tasteless food, the visibility and networking opportunities are unmatched. So chew that chicken, swallow hard, and smile. Those equally unimpressed people sitting across from you may very well hold the key to your next job. As for consultants, they can be a great medium for getting your name and number around to other companies. Consultants have nothing to lose by recommending a qualified candidate who is already using their services.

When the Fat Lady Sings

Even when you find yourself sitting across the termination desk with termination papers before you, you can still protect yourself. Here are a few ideas:

▪ *Take stock of what you will need to survive until you find another job.* Professional outplacement consultants have typically said that it takes one month for every $10,000 of salary to find a new job, but many now estimate it to be more like one and a half or two months. If you are leaving a $60,000-a-year job, that could translate into one full year of unemployment. What do you need for basic survival? A reliable car? Cash for necessities? Are there any pressing medical problems? Each of these can and should be dealt with immediately after you are laid off.

▪ *If you plan to purchase a car or take out a second mortgage on your house, move quickly.* If the company is paying you severance over a period of time, there is a good chance that you are still technically employed while it pays you. This should give you time to qualify for financing and make the necessary purchases. Of course, bear in mind that you may not have a paycheck for quite a while, so you don't want to overburden yourself with new bills.

▪ *Find out exactly how long your medical coverage will continue.* Make appointments with your doctor during that time and have any necessary work done. If it is something that will take more time than you have coverage, talk to the doctor or dentist about billing for the procedure upfront. Often if you explain your situation, the medical professional will try to schedule you before coverage expires. While it is true that federal legislation lets you extend your coverage for eighteen months after termination, keep in mind that depending on your current plan, it can be very expensive, approaching $600 or $700 a month for a family of four.

▪ *Negotiate a letter of recommendation from your employer at the time of layoff.* Many will agree to write a letter stating that you have been laid off through no fault of your own. If anything, seeing this in writing may make you feel better and assure any future employers that you weren't fired because of your performance on the job.

What it all boils down to is this: *Make yourself as portable as possible.* Increase your breadth of skills so that you can do many different jobs. Diversify your retirement investments so that the loss of employment won't jeopardize your future. Spread your political alliances over many different people inside the company. Increase your professional contacts outside the company so that people in other companies know your capabilities.

By making yourself more diverse and adaptable, you will be better equipped to handle whatever the future brings. If that future includes a layoff, you will have already opened many opportunities that would have otherwise been shut had you stayed within the boundaries of your job. By diversifying your skills and investments, you maximize your chances of surviving in a workplace that is increasingly toxic to those whose potential aims in a singular direction.

Part Four

No More Slash and Burn: Choices and Opportunities

Throughout this book, I have attempted to show the ineffectiveness of a layoff as a business management tool. What I haven't dealt with are the very real problems facing businesses in today's world that create the circumstances for layoffs in the first place. How does a company keep tight controls on the size, cost, and effectiveness of its workforce? What can be done in lieu of layoffs to help the ailing corporation retool its human resources?

In these final chapters, I look at the responsible choices facing corporations. In some limited cases, layoffs are unavoidable and necessary. In most cases, other management tools are more effective, and I describe a number of them in the following pages. Here I also explore examples of successful companies that have managed large numbers of employees and rejuvenated profits without a layoff. In the final chapter, "A New Social Contract," I present some ideas for how employees, the legal system, and society need to change to accommodate corporate competitiveness and provide dignity to the workforce.

12

The Toxic Prescription: When a Layoff Is the Only Option

As this book has shown most layoffs aren't effective for the companies that use them. Employees who survive a layoff suffer from diminished morale, loyalty, and productivity. The victims of a layoff lose their income and must fight an uphill battle to regain their standard of living. Communities and families are torn asunder by the ravages of a layoff, sometimes irreparably. Despite all of these negative side effects, there are times when a layoff helps a company survive.

There can be no doubt that layoffs are the toxic cure for American business and its workforce. Like a last effort to save the dying patient, sometimes a layoff is the only hope for recovery. When the organization starts to shudder with the mounting speed of a downward trek, drastic steps must be taken to salvage the company from the impending disaster. This is not preventative or preemptive. It is the last grasp for hope in the waning minutes while choices can still be made.

Laying off employees can bring relatively fast results, but only if the layoff is planned and executed for the *future* success of the company. All too often companies design a layoff around what executives think went wrong in the past, not what will ensure future success. That kind of layoff may be the final coffin nail for a division that could have been the cash cow of the future. Designing a layoff for the future requires conceptualizing the company's future before the first cuts are ever made. The effective layoff is a sign of a fundamental change in business strategy for the company, not purely a cost-cutting measure or, worse, a punitive correction aimed at poorly performing executives.

Justifiable Diagnoses

In general, there are only two organizational diagnoses for which a layoff brings relief. The first is when the organization has identical, repetitive operations in differing locations. Large chains of retail stores are susceptible to this diagnosis. These organizations create a store and then repeat that design many times in different locations. When sales are dangerously slow, closing the least productive of these identical stores can provide immediate relief with minimal damage to the organization. Some talent is lost in the layoff, but similar talent typically remains in the other identical operations.

More-complex organizations may also fall into this diagnosis. For example, one large furniture manufacturer opened several distribution centers across the country to service widely scattered showrooms that sold its products. Each distribution center was identical in operation and was designed to warehouse, distribute, and deliver inventory to the stores in the surrounding areas. When the price of wood doubled in 1994 and the furniture maket was in a slump, this manufacturer began to see a serious deterioration of revenues. To alleviate the financial crisis, the company closed the most distant distribution center, laid off all employees, and reassigned distribution activities to another center that was closer to the factory. The company discovered that it was cheaper to truck the merchandise to the more distant stores than to maintain a distribution center in that area.

The other diagnosis for which a layoff might be prescribed is when the company decides to shut down a particular line of business. This is an acknowledgment that the company is no longer competitive in some area of business and completely severs it from the organization. A layoff in this case involves firing all employees associated with the nonperforming business line. In this situation, the talent drain is minimized since the company will no longer need the talents and corporate knowledge that were necessary for the old business.

In both cases, the damaging side effects of a layoff on the organization are minimized. Because the layoffs are targeted at a specific location or line of business, the surviving employees retain a sense of control over their careers. These are not random, scattershot layoffs but are specifically aimed at areas of improvement. While there is still pain and loss, it is containable and less traumatic, and the loss of organizational skill and learning is minimized.

A company that used both of these layoff methods is Mervyn's, a West Coast–based department store chain. In the early 1980s, Mervyn's grew rapidly, opening more than 150 new stores throughout the southern and northwestern United States. By the mid-1980s, the company found itself in the paradoxical position of having grown too fast for its buying organization and distribution system to handle, and this growth spurt quickly reversed into a downward spiral. During a two-year period beginning in 1986, Mervyn's used both methods of layoffs to streamline its business. First, the company pulled its line of baby furniture, a business that was distribution heavy and with a low margin, and laid off all employees associated with the line. Because Mervyn's carries no other kind of furniture, the talent loss wasn't crucial, and the company was able to sever itself from something that had become a distribution nightmare. Second, the company shut its South-Central headquarters. Originally created to get closer to new customers in the South, it duplicated virtually every buying and management position at the corporate headquarters in Hayward, California. Reabsorbing a few of the South-Central employees, it laid off the majority. The strategic decision was not to expand as projected in that area of the country. Since the location was repetitive, the loss of talent was offset by counterparts at the California headquarters.

Layoff practitioners have a responsibility to practice their craft cautiously in a way that upholds the future success of the company and simultaneously respects the dignity of those whom they unemploy. Anything less is irresponsible malpractice. Unfortunately, layoff malpractice is common. Well-intentioned practitioners often err by doing what they think will protect the company but instead really does more harm than good. Here are just a few of the more common missteps in layoff malpractice.

Avoiding Layoff Irresponsibility

Malpractice 1: Allowing the Legal Department to Design the Layoff

Most companies are terrified at the prospect of litigation after a layoff. Stories abound (many of them true) of wrongful-discharge settlements that are in the hundreds of thousands of dollars (and in California, even in the millions), so the internal legal staff is often included in the first discussions of layoff strategy; in turn, staff attorneys often consult with labor law specialists, who outline all of the possible legal challenges to the layoff. Typically what evolves is an approach that is protective of the company from a legal stance but not necessarily good business strategy.

Most corporate attorneys will advise to lay off employees on a last-hired, first-fired basis equally across all departments. The most clearly defensible method for downsizing in a court of law is to lay off 10 percent of employees across all departments on a seniority-only basis. Under this approach, no one employee can claim that he or she was fired for discriminatory reasons. Furthermore, attorneys advise against saying anything more than what is absolutely necessary at the time of a layoff to both the departing employees and the survivors. This caution is designed to protect the company from making any implied or implicit promises. By strictly scripting what is said about the layoffs, the company is protected from emotional mis-speaks by managers who are stressed at having to let valued employees go.

Sound like a good approach? Only from a legal perspective. First, laying off employees by a flat percentage across different departments is somewhat irrational. How can it be that Accounting can do without the same proportion of employees as Human Resources? Could it be that one department can be externalized and the other left intact? The decision of how many employees should be laid off from each department should be based on an analysis of business needs, not the dictates of a statistical rule.

The concept of laying off employees strictly on seniority is also irrational. The choice of employees for a layoff should be based on a redistribution of the work, not the arbitrary date on which the employee was hired. An employee of eighteen months can be far more valuable than the one with eighteen years' seniority.

The scripted approach to layoff communications is also not a good idea. Certainly managers need to know what *not* to say, but a memorized script adds a cold and mechanical aspect to the act that makes it seem all the more reprehensible. This is a tough time for all employees, and they instinctively look to management for comfort and support for getting through it. When the manager refuses to discuss the issue and acts as if nothing has happened, employees are further alienated and angered. During layoffs, more than any other time, managers should be personable and approachable, not spouting some scripted message that treats employees past and present as if they were nonthinking imbeciles.

Legal counselors are paid to protect the legal interests of the company, and that objective may be at odds with the future success of the company. Although corporate attorneys should review the layoff approach, putting them in charge jeopardizes the surviving organization's health.

Malpractice 2: Giving as Little Notice as Possible

Out of a mix of fear and guilt, many executives choose to give employees as little forewarning as possible about an upcoming layoff. Certainly for good reason, managers fear that if employees know their fate ahead of time, they might become demoralized and unproductive, and maybe even sabotage the business. While all of this is a possibility, chances are it will happen with or without advance notice. In fact, there is no documented evidence that advance notice of a layoff increases the incidence of employee sabotage.

The *lack* of advance notice, on the other hand, dramatically increases the mistrust of management among the surviving workers. Trust is based on mutual respect. When employees discover what has been brewing behind their backs—and they will when the first person is let go—they see a blatant disrespect for their integrity, which completely destroys that trust. By not giving employees information that could be enormously helpful to them in planning their lives, management initiates a cycle of mistrust that can be enormously destructive of mutual trust—trust that can take years to reestablish.

Malpractice 3: Acting As If Nothing Happened

A widespread belief is that if not much is said about the layoff, everyone will put it out of their minds quickly. By acting as if nothing happened, managers assume that employees will follow their lead and get back to work, so discussions between employees and managers about feelings surrounding the layoff, although strongly encouraged by layoff consultants, are rarely conducted. Some managers, through explicit warning or implied gestures, discourage those who would express anything other than support for the company's actions.

But employees must talk about what has happened. If they aren't allowed to express their feelings in a protected and supportive environment, they will do it among themselves. The more their feelings are suppressed by the company environment, the greater the need will be to dwell on the trauma that has passed. And it only gets worse.

I don't advocate sessions where employees vent their spleen. Rather, recovery is hastened if managers and employees are allowed to speak honestly and fairly about what has happened. Tremendous support and encouragement can evolve among the work group that is allowed to process the changes thrust upon them. Acting as if nothing happened makes the trauma more painful.

Malpractice 4: Blaming the Scapegoat

There is only one thing more difficult than laying off an employee: taking responsibility for doing it. Managers often feel enormous guilt over having made the decision about who would be laid off. Facing the diminished team after the fact and admitting that you were the one who identified who would go takes courage. Sometimes it is easier to blame something or someone else for the decision.

The blame game has many players after a layoff. Sometimes senior management sanctions a corporate scapegoat to blame. The failure of a particular product, a previous senior management team, an unfavorable economy, the antics of a corporate raider—all of these and many more are reasons given for conducting a layoff. One West Coast company owned by a distant holding company blamed the unsuspecting parent company for the layoff, despite the fact that the whole idea was hatched by the company's CEO. Whatever the statement of corporate blame, it is invariably punctuated with proclamations of "we simply had no choice."

But the truth is that there was a choice, and everybody, including the employees, knows this. Sure, times may be hard and the cash running low, but there are always choices about what course of action to take. Somebody in senior management decided to conduct a layoff. When that person refuses to take responsibility for his or her actions, the morale of the surviving employees drops even lower.

This evasive tactic can start an unproductive cycle of blame within the organization. Very quickly, managers and employees learn that it is perfectly acceptable to blame a feasible target for failure. At a time when so many are motivated to protect their jobs, distancing oneself from failure becomes a survival technique. As a result, organizational politics become an unproductive skirmish of internal fault finding, which is about the last thing an ailing organization needs.

Layoff Standards

There are some standards to which layoffs of all types should adhere. These standards apply across the board and are the key to a successful layoff.

Too Much Profit or Too Many People?

The first and most important question that must be asked before any layoff is, "Is the need for this layoff driven by having too many employees, or too little profit?" If the answer is too little profit, this is the first warning sign that your company isn't ready for a layoff. Using a layoff as a cost-cutting measure is utterly foolish, akin to taking the engine out of your car because the car isn't working correctly. Sure, somewhere in that engine may be a problem, but removing it from the car doesn't help anything. The same happens with organizations contemplating a layoff. Throwing away valuable talent and organizational learning by dumping employees only makes a bad situation worse.

It the answer is "too many employees," there is a good chance that a well-thought-out strategy for change has been established for the organization. Products and services have been reworked and work flow has been reengineered. Only under these circumstances can a management team know that it has too many employees. Although most layoffs are the direct result of dwindling profits, it is the realization of too many employees that drives the successful layoff.

Define the New Company

A clear and well-defined vision of the new company is imperative before any layoff is initiated. Management should know what it wants to accomplish, where the emphasis will be in the new organization, and what staff will be needed. In short, the company should know exactly where it is going *before* it starts the process of downsizing.

The organization after downsizing will not be the same as it was before. Unfortunately, many managers underestimate the momentum of the old organization to recreate in the new one the same old problems. Unless there is a new concept of the business that is clearly understood and accepted by all the key players, the past will sabotage the future.

The vision of the new organization must come from the top down. Senior executives must both communicate the vision and act accordingly, sending a signal down through all branches of the organization that this change is for real. If the problems of the past are to remain in the past, an enacted vision of the new company must precede the restructuring.

Guard Adult Dignity

The methods employed in most layoffs treat managers and employees like children. Some things they are told and others they aren't because, it is said, "They can't handle it." Information is doled out in easily swallowed pieces. At the same time, a manager's control over his or her staff is completely violated. Often human resources staff step in and set rigid policies about who will be laid off and exactly how it should be done. Employees invariably see somber, tight-lipped human resources people huddling in meetings with their manager. Who's kidding whom here? The first phone call to the manager's secretary setting up the meeting has already set the organizational grapevine on fire. In an amazingly short time, those armchair strategists at the watercooler have tracked the unusual increase in human resources meetings. They know something is brewing.

Open and honest communication with middle managers is a must for a successful layoff. Trusting them to handle the situation like adults elicits adult behavior. Giving these managers a chance to work through all of the information provides them with a sense of control over what is happening.

Protecting the dignity of those who are laid off is critical. Using security guards to escort these employees from the termination meeting to the parking lot screams, "We know all of you employees really want to act like children and retaliate, so we are taking protective steps." The ultimate insult to the person who has spent years being loyal to the company is suddenly to be treated as an outsider and potential saboteur. Every surviving employee who witnesses this—and they all do—realizes how little respect the company has for loyal employees.

A layoff must guard the pride and confidence of those leaving. Some may want to leave quietly. Others may want to have a good-bye dinner with their coworkers. Some may need to delay the layoff until after closing on a house or other important personal transaction. The company should consider each situation and work with employees to allow a graceful exit. The rule of thumb here is to show laid-off employees the same respect shown them on the day they were hired.

Respect the Law

A number of laws apply to a layoff—both federal statutes like the Civil Rights Act, Age Discrimination in Employment Act (ADEA), Americans with Disabilities Act (ADA), Worker Adjustment and Retraining Notification Act (WARN) and state laws. California's right-to-privacy law, for example, has bearing on the manner in which a layoff is conducted. These laws are important and should be respected for what they *intend* as well as the specifics of their requirements.

The intent of the law is often quite clear. Under ADEA, treating employees over age 40 differently from those who are younger is clearly prohibited under the intent of this law. Similarly, the ADA is designed to protect employees with disabilities from disparate treatment in employment matters. Any layoff practice should uphold these intents.

Unfortunately, there are many ways to subvert the intent of these laws and still be in compliance. How? Here's one example. Charlie was employed by an insurance company for twenty-two years. During his twentieth year with the company he had a massive heart attack that caused him to be away from work for the better part of six months, creating a great hardship on the company, which relied heavily on Charlie to manage the field sales team. Charlie's company, in compliance with the law, did not allow him to return to work until after his doctor had written a letter saying that Charlie was completely recovered and could return to full-time work. A year later, the company, fearful that the heart attack was the beginning of a possible extended battle with heart disease, laid Charlie off. Although Charlie was completely recovered and had no limitations, company executives were uneasy about relying on him. Charlie's layoff was completely defensible according to the specific terms of the law but way out of line with the law's intent.

Any layoff practitioner has a moral and ethical responsibility to uphold the spirit of the laws that apply to employment. Although loopholes abound, the expertise of the practitioner is wrongly used when the layoff specialist becomes the loophole consultant. In additon, a clear respect for the law translates into respect for the company. When the company upholds the values of society, the society responds with respect and loyalty.

When a layoff is the only choice, it must be done with responsibility and planning. The best rules to guide layoff decisions are to do what is morally right, what is legally required, and what is in the best interests of the business. When these three criteria are met, the chances of success for the company and the work force, past and present, increase dramatically. When one or all are ignored, the cure becomes worse than the disease.

13

Alternative Strategies: Payroll Reduction Without Layoffs

Have you ever awakened on a workday morning only to realize that sometime during the night or early morning you had reached over and turned the alarm clock off? You scramble out of bed, your mind reeling as you realize that you have already missed thirty minutes of your boss's staff meeting. Thoughts of how you will explain your late arrival without looking irresponsible flood your mind as you race down the freeway toward the office. It's too late for anything but some serious damage control.

That is the same situation confronting many companies that face a layoff. The time for planning and prevention has come and gone. The point of no return into serious financial troubles has already passed. There are no options other than reducing the payroll—and fast.

As in the missed wake-up alarm, two scenarios emerge. One occurs the night before. That is the *prevention* period, when the next day's schedule is checked, the commute time calculated, and the alarm set to provide ample time to make the appointments. For companies, the prevention period happens several years before the need for a layoff surfaces. It involves several aspects, the foremost of which is melding the strategic business plan with individual career paths in a dynamic human resources plan. But once the alarm has sounded and the deadline has been missed, the opportunity for prevention and planning has long passed. The company is now solidly in the *reactive* period, when the search is for the least intrusive methods of immediate cost reduction. Even in this reactive period, most companies can trim their payroll without turning to a mass layoff.

In this chapter I look at what can be done to avoid a layoff in both the prevention and reactive phases. Since most companies looking for help are already well into the reactive stage, we'll start with the reactive methods for reducing the payroll without having to conduct a mass layoff. Then we'll examine what can be done in the prevention period to avoid such dire straits in the first place.

The Reactive Phase: Workforce Reductions Without Layoffs

The Hiring Freeze

The first and most obvious reactive technique is a hiring freeze, which relies on attrition for reductions in staff. The way it works is simple: Do not add new positions or replace employees who quit or retire. If the business has been in a downswing and the job market is healthy, there is a good chance that employee turnover has increased. By relying on attrition, you simply take advantage of a situation that is already occurring.

One key factor in making a hiring freeze successful is to allow for certain limited exceptions. The most important of all exceptions is to allow managers to rehire for positions vacated when an employee was fired for poor performance. If this exception is not made, managers will be hesitant to fire anyone for fear that they will not be able to hire a replacement—preferring a poor performer to nobody in the job. Other exceptions should be made for strategic projects. If the goal is to turn the business around, certain strategic departments will need to add staff. These departments should be identified and allowed to hire on a limited basis.

The hiring freeze method is extremely popular. Right and Associates found this method to be used by over 70 percent of companies needing to downsize. This method is the least obtrusive to organizational morale and commitment. While it is slower to reduce the payroll than other methods, it does so with the least negative side effects.

When BB&T Financial Corporation and Southern National Corporation merged in early 1995, they used a hiring freeze to minimize the number of redundant positions in the new organization. According to BB&T chairman John Allison, the use of attrition meant that "95 percent of the remaining work force will stay on when the new organization is formed." BB&T's use of attrition evolved out of the company's sense of loyalty to employees: "We have an obligation to take care of these people. We will do everything we can to help them find jobs and ease the transition," says Allison.

Reduced Hours and Plant Closures

Another technique, championed by the high-tech giant Hewlett-Packard, is the use of what HP internally called a "fortnight work schedule." That is, every two weeks (a fortnight) employees do not work for one day. When it was used during a slow sales period in August 1985, wages were cut 10 percent. Combining these savings with shutting the nonsales offices down during the Thanksgiving and Christmas holidays not only saved additional payroll dollars but recouped a generous amount by closing the facilities. To help employees handle the loss in pay, the company allowed qualifying employees to use vacation days during the forced time off so that there was no immediate loss in pay. In Europe, the giant automobile maker Volkswagen has been climbing back to profitability after having put many of its 100,000 workers on a four-day week. The company estimates that it has avoided laying off as many as 30,000 workers by using the reduced workweek.

Reducing hours is less diminishing to morale than other alternatives that I have suggested, because it plays to a sense of equity in the workers. Other methods of reduction seem to take something away and demand more, while this method takes something away but also requires less of the workers. The loss of pay may hurt, but the gained leisure time helps to remove the sting.

A related version of reducing hours, restricting overtime,

can be an effective means of reducing payroll in businesses with a large hourly workforce. Since overtime is paid at a considerably higher rate than regular time, the savings can mount up quickly. This method comes with a caveat: Many companies restrict overtime and then look the other way as employees continue to work off the clock. Not only is this illegal, but it can result in costly lawsuits and payment of back wages if these employees ever decide to bring litigation for the unpaid overtime.

Reducing Pay

Another common technique, reducing the pay for the same number of hours worked, often requires *all* employees to accept a 10 to 20 percent cut in wages. But experience shows this method to be one of the least beneficial ways to reduce the payroll. It almost always leads to a serious dip in morale and lowered productivity. Especially when the pay cut is permanent, many employees psychologically adjust their output to match the reduced wage.

Further, across-the-board pay cuts have been shown to drive the more skilled workers to find other jobs. Workers frequently see the pay cut as a warning sign of layoffs to come and start to anticipate the worst. And if the company retains a profit while employees are working under reduced wages, workers decide they are paying for the company to enjoy profits. All of this suggests that pay cuts are best done for a predetermined time period, returning to the normal wage after the specified time.

One method of reducing pay has been shown to work rather well in the short term. Instead of reducing pay across the board, the company ties the pay of its higher-paid managers and executives to overall company performance. If the company meets its financial objectives, the executives receive their full pay. If not, they receive a percentage of that pay dependent on the level of company performance.

The Wall Street giant Salomon Brothers is using this method to turn around a $500 million loss in 1994. More than 100 managing directors in Salomon's "client-driven business" receive base compensation equivalent to about 35 percent of their total compensation for 1994. If that business does not make money, that is all they get. If the client-driven business does make money, all the profit goes to the company until it has earned an after-tax rate return of 7 to 10 percent. Above that level, the managing directors in the business split 40 percent of the profit. Although it is too early to say if this has been effective, one thing is certain: Those managing directors are doing everything they can to make it work and earn their paychecks.

Voluntary Severance

Voluntary severance packages, which offer employees an amount of money for every unit of time they have been employed by the company, are probably the least invasive of all reactive techniques for reducing the payroll. Voluntary severance does carry a hefty price tag, but it is an effective way of reducing wages over the long term. For some employees, this is all the incentive they need to start their own business, go back to school, or strike out in some other new direction. The point is that a voluntary severance program gives the employees some control over their own destiny, preserving the trust of the remaining employees and giving those who leave a sense of dignity and self-confidence.

The list of companies that have effectively used voluntary severance programs is long and diverse. In 1994, Mayor Rudolph Giuliani used it to cut more than 7,600 employees from New York City's beleaguered budget. Raytheon offered packages to 4,000 employees in an effort to counteract a 10 percent drop in the company's defense-related businesses. In the early 1990s Digital Equipment Corporation tried to turn around its computer business profits by ousting 5,500 employees through a voluntary severance program. GTE, while spending $74 million to sever 6,400 employees, recorded an increased profit of $438 million in 1992.

Despite all the benefits of voluntary severance programs for downsizing, only a minority of restructuring companies offers them. One national survey conducted by the compensation consulting firm of Hewitt Associates found that only 42 percent of downsizing companies used voluntary severance packages as part of their reduction strategies. One reason for this slow adoption can be seen in what happened to Polaroid in the mid-1980s. The Cambridge, Massachusetts, company offered a lump sum—in some cases, as much as thirty months' pay—to employees who were willing to leave. In the end, the program was so successful that Polaroid had to hire replacements for many of those who left and even had to rehire some of the most valued employees who had been let go. Most companies, however, can expect 10 percent or less of their employees to accept a voluntary buyout, according to a recent survey by the management consulting firm of Wyatt and Company.

Early Retirement

Offering early retirement to those who are over age 50 can reduce the payroll of companies with an aging workforce. By loosening the requirements for retirement and easing the financial penalties on the employee, payroll expense can be reduced with few upfront costs. Many, if not most, employees who are approaching retirement will gladly accept a modest reduction in benefits for the addition of five or ten years to their retirement. As long as it is administered on a completely voluntary basis, this staff reduction technique is relatively harmless to the employee and the company.

Consider what would have happened to a 50-year-old, $50,000-a-year employee with twenty-five years of service at du Pont when it offered early retirement in 1992. Normally if this employee retired early, he or she would receive only $7,512 a year. But since du Pont waived the actuarial reduction for those who would leave early, the pension jumped to $18,756 a year— more than twice what it would have been and a very attractive offer to the 6,500 du Pont employees who accepted it.

As with voluntary severance, the effectiveness of early retirement programs hinges on voluntary offers. If pressure is brought to bear on employees to accept early-out packages, the perception of the program is the same as if it were a layoff. All of the organizational benefits gained by providing severance payments are lost when employees feel that they have lost control of their careers.

Each of these reactive techniques, though less than ideal, is effective for bringing immediate savings to the organization in imminent danger. But even when they are used, there is a larger unanswered question: What went wrong to cause such a problem? Why was management unable to plan and prevent these circumstances from the beginning?

Preventive Methods: How to Avoid Reductions Altogether

Applying Material Resources Planning to Human Resources

Several years ago while I was working with a client company on developing a human resources planning process, I was invited to attend a most unusual training program. The client, an industrial software firm, wrote and sold computer programs for managing just-in-time manufacturing processes. Now, I must admit that before I took this project, I never had much of an interest in manufacturing techniques and controls. This training program changed my mind.

The attendees were all professionals from various areas of the company. None of us had any experience with just-in-time, and the objective of the program was to familiarize us with the process in hopes that it would help us to understand the company's clients and their needs. The program was to last for three days, and I fully expected at the outset to spend that time plowing through a six-inch binder filled with flowcharts and diagrams. Boy, was I wrong!

For the first day, we were instructed to wear old clothes and meet in the cafeteria. When we arrived, the sixteen of us were split into four teams of four people. Much to our surprise and amusement, we were told that our task for the entire morning would be to bake cakes! When the laugher subsided, the instructor assured us that he was quite serious and gave us detailed instructions on how to make these cakes. He gave us a goal of completing twenty-three cakes in two hours.

I can't remember all of the specific instructions, but the upshot of it all was that we would be given four containers of vary-ing sizes, one mixing bowl, and six round cake pans. Our task was to order from the supply desk the necessary ingredients (eggs, cake mix, water, and oil) to make the cakes. The problem we had to solve was that the four containers we had been given could not hold all of the ingredients to meet our goal of twenty-three cakes. Therefore, we had to devise a plan for how much of each ingredient we would need and when it should be delivered to our workstation. Each team submitted this plan to the supply desk so the supply clerk could deliver the supplies to each team according to its plan.

Once the two-hour baking session began, everything went smoothly for the first two cakes. It was then, however, that we discovered we didn't have enough water to mix another cake, and according to our plan, we wouldn't be receiving any for another ten minutes. After we waited that out, we received an-other delivery of cake mix, but because we were behind sched-ule, we didn't have enough room in our container for the entire delivery. Thinking quickly, we grabbed some wax paper, formed a square on the desk, and had the remainder of the delivery dumped on that square. Now, with a greatly reduced working space, we continued with our baking frenzy.

I believe it was only a few minutes after the cake mix deliv-ery that we received our scheduled egg delivery. Of course, just as with the mix, we didn't have enough room in our container for all the new eggs, so we carefully placed them on the desk alongside the pile of cake mix. You can just imagine what hap-pened next: An egg rolled to the floor and broke, cake mix flew everywhere, we ran out of water *again,* and time slipped away. By the end of that two-hour fiasco, we had completed only eleven cakes, more than 50 percent below goal. If that wasn't bad enough, we had wasted two batches of mix and had an extra dozen or so eggs left over. Each of the other teams had similar results.

By the end of that day, we had learned in a very tangible way the value of just-in-time planning. Without proper planning and adequate tools for managing inventory, the cake bake was incredibly inefficient. We began to realize that no manufacturing operation could possibly be run the way we had run our little bakery. For the rest of the program, we learned the tools and techniques of just-in-time and how those sophisticated processes could forecast exactly what materials would be needed, how much, and when. At the end of the third day, we tried the cake bake exercise again, this time using our newly gained knowledge. At the end of that session, every team had met goal, and there was only a minimal amount of leftover inventory.

The concept of just-in-time has taken the manufacturing world by storm. Manufacturing managers around the world are all using this system to ensure that the right materials are present when they are needed. Suppliers are given detailed projections of what will be needed and when so that there is no need to store unnecessary inventory or pay the enormous overhead associated with a backlog of supplies. This kind of thinking has led many manufacturers, among them General Motors, to bring materials suppliers in-house. That way, they can become an integral part of the just-in-time manufacturing process.

If we can learn to be so efficient and sophisticated with materials inventory, why can't we do the same with human inventory, planning exactly what human capital will be needed to accomplish our objectives? Instead, we plod along with what we called in our cake bake exercise "Mama's way." Mama's way of baking a cake was to mix together the handfuls of ingredients she knew from memory would make a fine cake. When she found some ingredient missing, she would send one of the children to the store to pick it up. That's exactly what we do with our human resources. We hire "handfuls" of employees, hoping that we will have enough to meet the upcoming objectives of the business. If we find we haven't enough, we frantically call a headhunter and pay large amounts of money to buy the needed expertise. Similarly, if we find we have too many employees once the job is under way, we must resort to all of the measures mentioned earlier in this chapter or, worse, conduct a layoff. What manufacturing manager would keep his or her job with that kind of sloppy, laissez-faire operation? Yet most companies operate with just that kind of human resources planning.

Succession Planning: An Overview

The only way to prevent layoffs and other workforce reductions lies in adequate human resources planning. More specifically, it is the forecasting and planning of the "talent inventory" that occurs in succession planning. Succession planning is the ongoing process of creating a human resources plan that is based solidly on two factors: 1) the strategic plan of the company and 2) the skills and needs of employees. This is not the typical human resources plan that is rote bureaucracy and has little to do with the business forecast, the skills of employees, or accurate projections of manpower needs. Succession planning is a highly specific form of planning and forecasting which few companies do well.

Step 1: Assessing Employees

It begins with a thorough, accurate, and multifaceted assessment of every employee's performance and potential, based on a combination of information from many sources: the supervisor, coworkers, customers, suppliers, and the employee. It can be collected through various methods, from labor-intensive interviews to electronic surveys.

The assessment of employee performance and potential *is not* the same as the typical company performance review, which is done for compensation purposes. While the assessment of performance for succession planning and the typical assessment of performance for compensation are the same in concept, the difference between these two can be phenomenal. Why? Almost every company forces some sort of distribution on performance reviews for compensation. There is a limited budget for pay raises; there can be only so many high, middle, and low performers. The result of this forced distribution is that performance ratings are adjusted to fit the prescribed compensation distribution instead of accurately reflecting employees' performance. Typical performance reviews are further confounded by companies that dictate an employee's performance rating cannot be higher than his or her division's overall performance.

The only way that succession planning can be successful is to base it on *accurate* performance assessments. That assessment should cover the employee's past performance and not be forced into any compensation-determined distribution. The integrity of the entire succession plan relies on accurate and honest employee performance evaluations.

A second evaluation required in succession planning is an assessment of employee future potential. While assessments of potential are more difficult than performance assessments, they are also critical to the success of succession planning. The question of potential is how much promise does an employee show for increases in personal contribution, management, responsibility, and authority?

Sometimes an employee's performance assessment and potential assessment differ greatly. Some employees who have great potential for success find themselves in a job where they are unable to perform. Should they be fired because of circumstances that prevented them from really contributing? Careful analysis of the performance-potential differential can reveal some very valuable data about maximizing every employee's productivity.

One especially important factor in a successful succession planning system is honest employee feedback after these assessments of performance and potential are complete. All of the analysis and planning will have little effect if the employee isn't aware of where he or she fits in the future of the company. As a particular skill set becomes obsolete, the affected employees need to know it, so they can acquire skills that will be needed. Employees with low performance and little potential should be coached and carefully managed until improvement or an employment change occurs. Those with high performance but whose potential is low need to be aware that there are serious doubts about their future. Given that information they can begin to take steps to prevent obsolescence.

Step 2: Analyzing the Strategic Business Plan

After employee assessments, the second phase of succession planning requires careful analysis of the company's strategic business plan. What positions will be critical to the plan? What positions will no longer be needed? What skill does the company need for core businesses? What new lines of businesses will be created? What skills will these require?

This step of forecasting business requirements for human capital is potentially the weakest link in the process. This cannot be a guess. It cannot simply be today's head count with one or two positions added for good measure. It must be a thoughtful projection of talent needs based on the work to be performed. There are any number of project management tools, techniques, and software available to assist the manager in making this forecast accurate.

Success in this phase of planning lies in holding managers responsible for the accuracy of their forecasts. Unfortunately, management accountability for inventory and capital is often given more importance than accountability for the human talent inventory. For example, I know one high-level manager who has his secretary fill out each year's human resources plan by copying the previous year's plan and simply updating a few of the objectives. This is hardly a recipe for accurate and thoughtful projections. If, however, his own performance rating hinged on the accuracy of that forecast, you can be assured that much more time and analysis would go into the making of that plan, but as long as it is regarded as more of that "HR red tape," the human resources planning process will never succeed.

Step 3: Managing Talent and Jobs

The next step in succession planning involves the matching of employee assessments and career goals with the strategic business plan of the company. The results can then be used to manage the business and to help employees find the best place for their skills in the organization. The ideal, maximizing each employee's skills and interests in a position that is part of the strategic plan, may be impossible to attain, but using it as a goal continually reshapes the workforce as the strategy of the company changes.

This kind of succession planning manages pools of talent and jobs rather than matching a candidate's skills to specific job requirements. For years, succession planning as it was practiced was nothing more than replacement charting. Every management job was reviewed once a year, and a tightly defined job analysis was matched to individual skills with the result being a replacement list for each position. The final product was an organization chart that listed beneath every job title and incumbent a slate of qualified replacements. In today's quickly changing business environment, this method of succession planning is not only too rigid but is forcing the companies that practice it into obsolescence.

Hiring for Tomorrow's Criteria

By matching candidates to hiring criteria for today's job, we are hiring based on *yesterday's* needs. Predicting the future by looking at the past was good strategy in a stable and consistent climate, but in this time of unparalleled change, it no long works. Jobs can change overnight—sometimes radically in just the time a job requisition is sent to the recruiter and when the final candidate is selected. Finding the ideal candidate for the well-studied and fine-tuned job description can mean promoting an employee who was a good fit for yesterday's job but a misfit in tomorrow's organization.

This became clear to me when I met a young woman on the rooftop patio of a friend's house in San Francisco shortly after the earthquake in 1989. Looking out over the quilt of Victorian row houses that cover the hills down to the bay, I couldn't help but think of the devastation of the earthquake and fire and how lucky those of us who live in San Francisco were that there wasn't more of this beauty destroyed. I chattered on about this to my acquaintance and asked where she was when the earth began to move. She referred to an industrial park down in Silicon Valley some forty miles south of San Francisco, the same industrial park where I had been during the quake. Knowing that my company was the sole tenant, I realized we had something in common.

"So what do you do?" I inquired.

Her face flushed, she stuttered, then said with a twist of sarcasm, "I don't know."

As she continued I wasn't sure if it was anger or just embarrassment that oozed between her words, but in any case, her anxiety was more than evident.

"I was hired two months ago to work in artificial intelligence after finishing my Ph.D. The company moved me, my husband, and our two children down from the Northwest to take an engineering position in the Manufacturing Productivity Division [MPD]."

Did I know of the MPD, she queried? I began to feel a bit sheepish and tried to muster my best poker face to hide my own guilt. Not only did I know of the MPD, I had been involved in its downsizing two months earlier.

She continued, "By the time I arrived, not only did the job not exist but the whole department had been disbanded!"

She was then placed in another job in the company's highly regarded research and development laboratory, only to hear the announcement two weeks later that the lab was abandoning all internal research on artificial intelligence and her job was eliminated. So now, in the course of two months, she was looking for job number three.

This story illustrates with poignancy the need for using the business strategy when hiring and promoting. If there is no consideration of the jobs that will be needed tomorrow, there can be no planning of what talents should be groomed to fill those jobs. Strategic succession planning is critical to reducing the waste of human capital that occurs in a layoff. When someone in management is planning for the future of employees, there is less of a need for dramatic changes when that future becomes a reality.

The human carnage from all our well-intended and best-designed reengineering efforts is not just piling up at the unemployment office but is choking the payrolls as well. Like the story of this engineer, many talented and motivated employees are hired to meet job descriptions that because of internal or external changes have transformed themselves into something entirely different. Because no one planned for these changes, employees are caught as misfits in a system that no longer has a place for them.

The Casualties of Change

The casualties of organizational systemic change are forced to make a choice. They either retread into other, more needed careers (for which they may have little interest or skill), cling to the old job until a layoff puts them out of work, or find another job that uses their skills. Consider a few examples.

The Obsolete Store Manager

John had been a manager of various sizes and types of stores for all of his thirty years in retailing. His strengths were in merchandising: spotting sales trends and displaying merchandise accordingly. Good merchandising is truly an art form, and not everyone has the knack for it. Knowing what merchandise will be hot this season and displaying it in such a way that it catches customers' eyes takes experience and a lot of intuition. For the three companies John had worked for, his ability to merchandise always put him among the top sellers—that is, until about five years ago.

In the mid- to late 1980s a technology revolution hit the retail industry, and John's job, dramatically: point-of-sale scanning. Scanning—the process of electronically reading bar codes at the checkout counter—is much more than just a convenience for the sales clerk; it records a volume of information about the product being sold and about the customer buying it. It allows a computer to register things like the style, color, price, and size of product being sold, as well as which products are typically purchased together by the same customer. In most cases, this information can be accessed with up-to-the minute accuracy at any time, so the store manager can review sales patterns and rearrange the merchandise display, pricing, and so forth to match that day's trends. No longer is the gut feeling of the store manager the deciding factor in merchandising. Careful analysis and solid business management are necessary for success.

John has been slow to use the new merchandising systems, and when he does, he doesn't understand much of what it tells him. He has been slipping in the sales ranks, even though he tries to keep up by working longer hours and spending much more time on the sales floor than he used to. He has become increasingly frustrated with what he sees as "home office interference" and thinks that the company has lost its focus on retailing.

Recently John's district manager demoted him to a smaller job.

Yesterday's HR Information Systems Manager

In the world of information systems and true programmers, there is probably no more despised person than the human resources information systems manager. Why? Because of the constantly changing complexity of HR systems. Tracking employee information, salary ranges, raises, bonuses, and benefits is tough enough, but add to that changing salary structures, bonus schedules, and benefit plans, and you have a recipe for organized chaos. It's no wonder that most management information systems (MIS) departments run and hide whenever human resources calls!

Don, the HR information systems manager for a company of 50,000 employees, holds the job that bears the brunt of HR system demands and coordination with MIS. He is a programmer by training and has many years of experience with large mainframe databases. Over the years he has learned how to tease almost any kind of request from his mainframe HR databases. In recent years, however, the need for Don's technical expertise has dropped with the rise in the use of personal computers, along with more sophisticated and easy-to-use systems. And now Don's boss has started making requests of him that he feels are outside his job. His boss is prodding him for a proactive information strategy. He feels Don should be spending his time planning for what information the various HR departments will need to do their jobs better and more efficiently in the future rather than troubleshooting systems. Don thinks that his job is to solve system problems, not to think through another department's business issues. He longs for the challenge of the old days when he could get his hands around a tough programming puzzle.

Both John and Don were hired to do a very specific job that they were well qualified for—that is, until those jobs started to change. Then both of these hardworking and successful employees found themselves increasingly unequipped, and perhaps even a bit unwilling, to stay up with the changes. The skills they were hired for and on which their pay was based are now obsolete. If they can, they must retool for the jobs they already have. If they can't or won't, they become stumbling blocks in a system that is ever evolving and transforming itself to adapt to the rapid changes of the business environment.

Assessing Skills for Tomorrow

If organizations are to maintain success into the future, managers have an obligation to acquire, develop, and promote talented people who will be likely to survive the many iterations of change the future will undoubtedly hold. But how, you ask, are we to hire employees who can do today's job *and* who are equipped for tomorrow's job—a job that we haven't even seen? I have found in my work of assessing and hiring many successful managers that four skills areas are key to determining success in tomorrow's jobs.

Broad Technical Knowledge

This is an age-old "forest versus the trees" paradox: We must shift our focus from hiring tree specialists to hiring those who know their way around the forest. It used to be that a good hiring decision was based on hiring the candidate who was the most specialized in the area of the job. If you were hiring a manufacturing manager, you wanted to hire a candidate skilled at the specific manufacturing and inventory process your company used. If you were hiring a programmer, you wanted an expert in the programming languages in which your applications were written.

Hiring candidates based on broad technical skills means hiring a manufacturing engineer who is well grounded in many approaches to manufacturing and a programmer who understands the basics of programming in many different languages. Maybe a candidate who doesn't even know your special process or language is the right one because he or she has a broad technical background in the area and can easily move among many specific techniques as needed.

Organizational Competencies

Every successful organization has certain core competencies—key areas in which the organization provides value to customers, who come to know the organization by these competencies and expect them in products and services. Some organizations are best at making reliable products, being the lowest priced, having the fastest turnaround, or having the most technologically advanced product. Whatever those two or three core competencies of the organization are, good hiring decisions should be based, in part, on the candidate's ability to provide that competency.

I once consulted with a company that is world renowned for making revolutionarily different computer products. That company's culture is saturated with the love of being outside the mainstream of the high-tech world, and its products reflect this stance. Their customers, often in creative professions, rely on being able to do the unexpected and to be at the forefront of change. When these loyal customers buy one of this company's computers, they expect it to be able to perform differently from all the rest.

Several years ago, this company needed to hire a training director, and searched for well over a year, unable to find a suitable candidate. During that search, they successively hired two candidates who were well trained and experienced in traditional training methods but lacked the ability to be truly creative in their work. Both left the job within a year. The candidate they did successfully hire was an ex–drama teacher turned M.B.A. who had a reputation for anything but traditional classroom-style training.

By hiring individuals who are consistent with organizational competencies, you increase the likelihood that these individuals will be suited for the organization in the future. Even as many things about the organization change to meet the market, the core competencies endure and remain central. Employees who share those ideals and have the skills necessary to perform them are more likely to be able to contribute to the success of the organization in the future.

Management Skills

Although many things about most organizations have and will change, one never will: the need to manage the work. Management skills transcend all other categories of work and professions and are an integral part of every successful organization. The term *management skills* includes not only managing the work flow of others, but more important, the ability to organize and manage one's own workload. By selecting employees who are experts in management, you strengthen the company's ability to pilot itself through whatever the future might bring.

Volumes have been written on how to hire a good manager, much of it tedious and not particularly useful. Basic management skills are relatively easy to spot, even in the candidate who has never "managed" or held a full-time position. To start with, look at how the candidate has managed the information flow during the interview. Is the resumé organized in a clean, efficient, and focused way, or is it a hodgepodge of personal information, much of it irrelevant to this person's ability to do the job? Has the candidate come to the interview prepared with questions designed to elicit a clear picture of the organization and the job requirements? These are just a few of the simple telltale signs of a good manager.

For more experienced candidates, it is always a good idea to ask specific behavioral questions about people and projects he or she has managed in the past. Questions that inquire about specific incidents—how a tight deadline was met, how a particularly stressful situation was managed, or how a problem employee was coached—usually give good information about the ability of the candidate to manage the work of others.

Learning Skills

Learning skills, that is, a willingness or motivation to learn, are critical to the success of tomorrow's employees. Candidates who have these skills will grow and learn with changes as they happen. As the job changes, these employees will be challenged to learn and master those changes. In the process, they will ensure their own success and the success of the organization.

Like management skills, the signs of learning skills are abundant and easy to assess. How did the candidate handle an unexpected academic challenge? Has the career path been linear (all in one well-defined line of work) or like a spiral (have there been some lateral moves that have expanded the candidate's repertoire of experience)? What education has the candidate sought out on his or her own after beginning his or her career?

Once while seeking to fill a position on my staff, I interviewed a fellow who had taken a year and a half off from his career to study piano at a local music conservatory. He had an otherwise glowing resumé and excellent references, so I wondered why he had chosen to take this unusual diversion. When I inquired about the time off, he told me of his lifelong desire to perfect his playing and how he had seized the opportunity at the time of receiving a small inheritance. Typically, this kind of hole in a resumé is viewed as a sign of a lack of commitment to career or, worse, of instability. But to the interviewer looking for learning skills, it can be a sign of someone who has a driving desire to learn, to be challenged, and perhaps to even grow to a new level of personal competency. Without a desire to learn and the skills to do so, the employee of the future will quickly be trampled by the pace of technological change.

Training: The Best Alternative to Specialization

Employee training is the solution for acquiring technical expertise in specialized areas. The organization must take responsibility for providing specialized training to employees on an as-needed basis. Employees can be taught highly specific technologies through mentoring with in-house experts, internal and external training courses, and self-study options made available through interactive media. By hiring and promoting employees with broadly based skills, the company will have versatile employees who can master new technologies quickly and easily.

Virtually any company, in any location and with a very small budget, can provide this kind of training. One alternative is through continuing education programs. An increasing number of nationally respected universities and private training companies are offering interactive training via satellite hookups.

Once the sole domain of National Technology University, there are now countless programs on virtually any topic available to employees, often without leaving their desks. Many of these programs are accredited and offer advanced degrees.

Another inexpensive and viable alternative is the use of self-study learning centers. There are many excellent training programs available on video or CD-ROM and as written media. Many of these can be rented from third-party distributors for a fraction of the cost of buying them.

Vendors of new technologies often have large training divisions that will, on request, train employees on the latest advances in the field at little or no cost to you. Where else could you get better information than from the people who invented it?

Building In a Capacity for Change

This approach to succession planning builds into the organization the capacity for change. Rather than trying to teach stranded employees change management, this approach advocates hiring employees who are already equipped to make the needed transitions. By helping these employees to fine-tune their skills through training, the organization "grows" specialization as opposed to hiring it.

As long as we continue to hire finely tuned employees to well-studied jobs, we run the risk of pushing the organization into talent obsolescence. The days of a static job knowledge, skills, and abilities are gone forever. The increased pace of information and organizational change has wrought many benefits, but it also demands that organizations be staffed with employees who can respond to that change.

Layoffs are not an adequate response to change. The cycle of staffing up and laying off that has plagued so many companies does nothing but siphon off critical momentum that could be used for beating the competition. The truly successful companies of the future will know the secret of strategic succession planning. They will have learned to plan as carefully and thoroughly for the movement of their human assets as they do the physical assets.

14

Choosing Controlled Growth: Changing Reality to Fit Vision

A New Way to Watch TV

The machine we have now come to call a VCR has been around since 1954. That's when Ampex Corporation built the first magnetic tape machine capable of recording video images. Large as a jukebox and more expensive than most cars of the day, it recorded images and sound—a real breakthrough in technology.

Those early VCRs were sold primarily to television stations and film studios that could afford them and had the personnel who could figure out how to run the monsters. Then in 1970 Sony unveiled a smaller version of the machine that used what was labeled a U-matic tape cassette and sold well. By 1975, it was believed that the market for video recording devices had leveled off.

One Japanese company, JVC, had a different idea—to bring these video recording devices into every home—and it went to work on making a machine geared to the average consumer. According to the design objectives, the machine had to connect to an ordinary television and provide the same quality image and sound as regular broadcasts, not be too expensive, be easy to operate, and have a minimum recording time of 2 hours (to accommodate the typical length of most motion pictures).

In 1974, Sony rushed a home machine to the market, but the Betamax was heavy, clumsy, and expensive. Two years later, JVC brought out a lighter, easier-to-use machine with sixty minutes more of recording time than the Betamax, and, it was considerably cheaper.

With all these features, you would have expected JVC's VCR to have caught on quickly. Well, it didn't. But despite year after year of slow sales, JVC continued pushing its VCRs in the market and licensing the technology to other manufacturers. After twenty years of commitment to the product, the VCR finally caught on in the 1980s. Sales of all brands of VCRs in 1993 alone exceeded 43.4 million units with a respectable share of that going to JVC—a wonderful triumph after two decades of bucking the odds.

Post-it, Please

Everyone today appreciates the simple beauty of 3M's Post-it notepads. What they may not know is that those little jewels almost didn't make it to the market. Back in 1964, a 3M engineer, Spencer Silver, was experimenting with new polymers for adhesives when he made a mixing mistake that produced an adhesive that was not "aggressively" tacky. The new adhesive was interesting to the researchers but deemed to be of little product value.

The idea for Post-it notes hit Silver ten years later while he was singing in the church choir. Marking the songs for that Sunday's service with little slips of paper, it occurred to him to use the adhesive on the slips to ensure that they would continue to hold their place. After five years of pushing the idea around 3M, the Post-it product was finally put into production and test-marketed in 1978. During that year, 3M introduced a number of new adhesive and tape products, so the Post-it didn't get any special treatment.

When the test market data showed the product hadn't sold, Silver was perplexed. Then it occurred to him: You have to use Post-it notes to appreciate them. The typical test market at 3M in those days didn't provide much incentive to use the product before purchase, so Silver packed his bags and took several hundred cases of the notes to one of the test market cities, Richmond, Virginia. There he and a colleague stood on the streets of the business district and passed out free samples of Post-its. In no time, the passersby were asking for more of these unusual notepads. Taking the results back to 3M, the company launched a campaign to send out free samples, and the rest is marketing history. Today no home or office is without them.

The Lessons Learned

What, you might ask, do VCRs and Post-it notes have in common? Besides being products that we use every day, they illustrate how two companies changed reality. Both companies had products that had never existed before, that didn't catch on at first, and that took unique marketing campaigns. These companies looked at the world outside of what existed at the time and imagined what could be—and then they went to work making it happen. Before it was over, the rest of the world's reality changed to fit *their* vision.

These two companies and their products illustrate one of the most powerful principles of human existence: Reality is often a product of the way you see it. When you see yourself as successful, you behave confidently and create an image that generates success. When a company sees opportunities for growth and development, it behaves in ways that make that growth a reality. When the company chooses to see those same opportunities as nonproducing liabilities and cuts them from the organization, that too creates a new reality—one that never realizes those lost opportunities.

A World of Paradigms

A paradigm is a set of rules that establishes boundaries and tells how to behave in order to attain success. It is a way of doing things—a set of assumptions about reality—that determine how we should think and behave. Paradigms are all around us, affecting our lives on a daily basis. Sports, professions, religions, and cultures are all paradigms; each defines boundaries of what is acceptable and gives the rules for success.

One of my favorite illustrations of the power of paradigms comes from a speech that psychologist George Kelly gave to a group of the American Psychological Association. In his speech, Kelly proclaimed that if Christopher Columbus had been a scientist, he would never have discovered the New World. There was nothing in the literature of the day to indicate that the world was anything but flat; had he forged ahead with such an insupportable investigation, he would have been utterly disappointed and defeated. Upon arrival in the New World, he would have realized that his hypothesis of sailing around the world to India had not been confirmed, and he would have returned, a failure among his colleagues.

Paradigms have tremendous impact on everything from science to corporate management. In business, there are strong, rigidly held paradigms about what kind of management and business strategy will bring success. Business schools are the bastions of this paradigm, teaching the rules of the game to new recruits before they enter the playing field. Under the reign of this paradigm, certain actions are also rewarded by Wall Street analysts and shareholders who cling to the paradigm's tenets. It is the magic of the self-fulfilling prophecy at work: Everyone expects certain actions to bring success; they respond accordingly, and this response helps create the very success they expect.

Over the years, two general paradigms have dominated the business world: the paradigm of the entrepreneur, which is based on growth and risk, and the paradigm of bureaucracy, focused on control and organization. Both continue to play useful roles for managers who are trying to navigate the treacherous waters of today's business environment; they offer direction and guidance in an otherwise chaotic and directionless storm.

These two paradigms, entrepreneurship and bureaucracy, operate in different realms. Entrepreneurship reigns among small businesses and individuals who are constantly looking for ways to grow and expand. This paradigm has a distinctive bootstrap quality that is rooted in the philosophy of taking what exists and is accessible, changing it in some useful way, and then making a profit off the sale. The entrepreneurship paradigm has few rules about organization or control. Instead, its focus is on growth and expansion.

The bureaucratic paradigm, on the other hand, is the dominant paradigm of almost every large organization. Despite the valiant attempts of many in the corporate realm to reject it, this paradigm continues to rule and regulate the actions of large organizations. Volumes have been written on the bureaucratic paradigm, mostly focusing on its negative attributes. But the truth is that the bureaucratic paradigm persists because it has some useful characteristics that help large, unwieldy corporations survive. Despite plenty of bad press, bureaucracy is not all bad.

The Rules of Reduction

In recent years, the bureaucratic paradigm has incorporated a set of rules regarding organizational size and layoffs. It is a reductionist approach, valuing smaller rather than larger and profits over growth. The rules of reduction began to arise during the recession of the early eighties and have slowly integrated into the bureaucratic paradigm. Now, regardless of overall economic conditions, the rules of reduction are accepted and practiced. Here are some of the key assumptions underlying the reduction rules of bureaucracy:

Leaner Is Meaner

Taken from the usual sports and military inventory of macho analogies that are so popular among corporate managers, this phrase, "getting lean and mean," has been overused to justify uncountable corporate butcherings. The assumption is that a reduced organization is more agile and flexible in the marketplace. Based on the idea of a lean street fighter who is quick and light on his feet, this suggests that reductions in force will somehow do the same for an organization.

Despite the catchy logic to this phrase, it isn't always true. Sure, an overstaffed organization is usually slower to respond to change, but a slimmer organization, especially one that has just gone off a crash diet, isn't necessarily any better prepared to handle change. In many cases, just the opposite is true because the organization struggling to survive after a massive layoff tends to turn attention inward to restructuring, taking its eye off the market and critical changes. Furthermore, the trauma of the layoff often compels the organization to avoid any further changes until it can regain its balance and perspective.

Costs Are More Predictable Than Revenue

This assumption is more subtle than the others but equally influential. Many managers automatically and uncritically assume that the future costs of doing business are predictable and controllable. Future revenue, on the other hand, is seen as less predictable and controllable. Consequently, one of the rules of reduction is to control what is controllable rather than speculating about what isn't. Since the two basic ways to increase profit are to cut costs or increase revenue, this rule directs managers to look for costs to cut.

The fact is that future revenue is just as predictable as future costs. Although forecasting future sales takes more work and thought than adding up the bills, it can be done effectively. Trend analysis, based on past revenues, can often estimate future income. Beyond the technology, the real problem here lies with senior managers who give greater credence to proposals about cutting costs than those about growing revenue.

The Percentage of Cuts Equals the Percentage of Savings

This assumption is that if the company cuts 10 percent of its payroll, it will eventually realize that 10 percent in savings. The logic is simple and linear: If I stop spending by a certain amount, I should start retaining that same amount in my account.

Once again, this simplistic and beguiling reasoning doesn't hold up. Cutting costs, especially with a layoff, is a complex and curvilinear problem. When cuts are made in an organization, the effect on the reduction of costs is an accelerating function. Small cuts have little effect; they may not even make a dent in the bottom line. Larger cuts may have a small effect but usually not nearly as large as the percentage of cut. Deep, large-scale cuts can bring immediate and large savings to the books, but only temporarily, and they may jeopardize the future of the organization.

Cutting Jobs Will Force Workers to Work Smarter

This assumption might otherwise be worded, "Necessity is the mother of invention." The senior management team that wants to force workers to abandon their clumsy, inefficient ways might come to the conclusion that reducing the head count but not reducing productivity expectations will force workers to work smarter. If the surviving workers want to keep their jobs, it is reasoned, they will have to learn to do more with less.

This commonsense assumption fails to produce because it disregards one of the fundamental truths about people under extreme stress: They do what they have always done, only now they do it faster and harder. The worker who survives the layoff and must now work under the stress of greater demands with less help is not likely to take the time and risk involved in re-thinking the way he or she does a job. Instead, he or she focuses on the increased workload and tries to accomplish it with the same behaviors, only accelerated. While this increase in productivity may be helpful for a while, it is new and more efficient behaviors that are needed for sustainable change. Working *smarter*, not *harder*, is what makes a difference.

Layoffs create an anti-risk-taking environment. Keeping your head low, working hard at what you've always been successful at, and avoiding failures at all costs is the most common response of a surviving worker to a layoff. Trying new and un-proved methods holds great potential for failure—failure that could make one the next candidate for a layoff.

Cost Cutting Is a Strategic Business Plan

Ailing companies have a hard time not thinking about their troubles. Getting out of pain becomes a fixation, one that is all consuming. Consequently, the five-year business plan of a company in the red often has very little of real substance other than cutting costs. The corporate planners go to great lengths to show how cost cutting will lead the company to a brighter future and say precious little about tapping new markets with new products and services.

Cutting costs is not a strategy for healthy business. It may be a necessary element of any business plan, but it is not in and of itself a path of to the future. It is akin to saying that one's New Year's resolution to use more coupons will be the secret to living a full and happy life. Cost cutting does have its place, but it is effective only when coupled with fundamental plans to do business differently. There must be some blueprint for growth that allows the business to move past the situation where it is stuck. Without a plan for change, the costs almost always return, and corporate life becomes a continual downward spiral.

Mature Markets Exist

Forget what you learned in business school; the concept of the mature market is a myth. Simply put, when one company abandons a growth strategy in a "mature" market, another firm almost always appears with new ideas and products that expand and renew the market.

The ever-popular personal computer is a case in point. When Steven Jobs and Steve Wosniak approached the electronics giant Hewlett-Packard with their idea of manufacturing a personal computer, HP turned them down flat. The home electronics market was small and narrow, consisting of mainly young, wannabe electronics engineers. There just wasn't enough potential revenue there to warrant HP's investment.

Six years later, Jobs and Wosniak were heading Apple Computers, which had earned each of them in excess of $100 million making—what else?—personal computers. Both HP and IBM had turned down similar ideas, and both lost a critical lead in the market that ultimately cost both companies billions of dollars in lost revenue.

The assumption that markets mature is a grave error of the bureaucratic paradigm. According to this concept, if everything stays constant, there can be no growth in revenue with this product or service in a particular market. But think about it: How many products do you know of in today's market that stay constant? One inspired improvement, perhaps even a simple re-packaging or feature redesign, can change the sales picture dramatically. History proves that companies that stop growing and developing in a market do not stand still; they always lose.

Dangerous Cuts

The rules and assumptions about reduction that have been inte-grated into the bureaucratic paradigm are dangerously faulty. These assumed truths have permitted business leaders to make uncritical cuts in businesses that are in desperate need of rejuve-nation, not dismemberment. We will never know how many VCRs and Post-its have been lost to the narrow reality of the reduction paradigm.

NYNEX, for example, will sack an extraordinary 16,800 workers between 1994 and 1997, hoping to save $1.7 billion, $40 million of which it has agreed to pay Boston Consulting Group for helping with the layoffs. But even *The Wall Street Journal* ques-tions these cuts as going too far, perhaps going beyond fat and into the bone. So does New York State's attorney general, who has argued that NYNEX service ranks the lowest of all forty tele-phone companies operating in the state. The reduction mentality is leading this company into questionable territory and perhaps even destroying the very services it provides.

The argument that the reduction mentality accounted for the swift growth in the 1980s just doesn't hold up according to the latest Census Bureau analysis. The study, based on detailed, nonpublic corporate disclosures in the economic census, which is taken every five years, found that labor productivity fell in more than one-third of the companies that laid off workers be-tween 1977 and 1987. The survey also found there were just as many successful "upsizers" as there were successful downsizers during that period, suggesting that downsizing may be limiting productivity growth rather than improving it.

The Controlled Growth Paradigm

It is time for a new paradigm—one that combines the best of both the entrepreneurial growth paradigm and the carefully controlled and managed bureaucratic paradigm. This new, hybrid framework—the controlled growth paradigm—will be critical for the long-term success of American business.

The new paradigm changes some basic assumptions and rules, as all new paradigms do. It sets new boundaries for what is expected of all the constituents of the corporate world. Changing the paradigm transforms the highly destructive forces of corporate reductionism into a force for the good of the company, and ultimately investors, without the senseless destruction of corporate assets.

Quarterly Reports of Profit Are Not Healthy Guideposts for Growth

The excessive importance and overinterpretation given to quarterly financial statements by management and investors is the most damaging practice of big business today. Quarterly reports are anxiously awaited by investors who are looking for a faster return on their investment. Are revenues up but profits down? Sell immediately. The company's stock price tumbles. Are revenues and profits up? Buy more shares and force the company stock price to new highs.

Admittedly this is a simplistic analysis of the stock market, but it is the fundamental trend of quarterly financial reporting. Senior managements shudder at the thought of reporting even a single quarter of poor performance, and several consecutive poor quarters can cut the market value of the company by a half or more as investors move on to greener pastures. Corporate management is hypersensitive to this trend and avoids releasing a poor quarterly report at all costs.

The selling of company assets to boost income is just one of the many sleight-of-hand tricks company management pulls to hide poor performance. Another is to release a poor quarterly report and simultaneously announce the layoff of large numbers of employees. Layoffs always attract lots of press, spreading the message that company management is taking "proactive" steps to turn around the poor performance.

The effect of overinterpreting quarterly reports reminds me of the childhood story about the blind men and the elephant. As the story goes, three blind men were each allowed to touch one part of the elephant. One was given the trunk, one the belly, and one the tail. Each of the men came up with completely different descriptions of an elephant, none even remotely close to a real elephant.

So it is with quarterly reports. Sometimes a company on the path of a long-term strategy must endure several poor quarters—or even years—to reach the point of sustainable success. If any one of these quarterly reports were taken outside the context of the longer-term strategy, it would appear as if management were failing and the company was a poor investment. When the whole of the strategy is considered, the poor quarters become inconsequential to the company's long-term success.

In February 1995, Geneva Overholser, the editor of the *Des Moines Register* for six and a half years, resigned from what is often called one of American's finest newspapers because of her publisher's preoccupation with quarterly reports. "I wish we could concentrate on making money by putting out a good newspaper, instead of trying to satisfy shareholders on a quarter-to-quarter basis." The paper is published by Gannett, which has gained a reputation for cost efficiency and garnered high marks from cost-conscious Wall Street.

The controlled growth paradigm must diminish the importance of quarterly reports. Of far greater importance to investors, company management, and employees is the company's overall strategy. A company with great performance that is riding the wave of a changing market but has no business strategy for the future is not a cash cow but a problem about to erupt. Tolerance and room for maneuvering are required for any company that seeks steady, solid, and continuous success.

Hiring of Permanent Employees Is an Ongoing Capital Investment

In spite of all the good the accounting profession has given to the corporate world, it has contributed one idea that is nearly choking the life out of many organizations: that employees should be viewed as liabilities. This accounting principle has fostered a virtual contempt for payroll expenses and fuels the many expeditions to reduce this human liability in every way possible.

Under the current reductionist paradigm, employees are seen as an expense—a consumable commodity. You buy the people power you need to keep the business running. When you discover that you have more people than you need, you stop buying as many. Employees are interchangeable components that can be plugged in wherever and whenever they are needed. They are disposable as well. When the immediate demand for their services has subsided, they can be discarded.

To evaluate this point, Henry Kelly and Andrew Wyckoff of the federal Office of Technology Assessment compiled a study showing that the statistics government uses to measure corporate spending are wildly skewed. Government statistics treat spending on the intellectual capabilities of the workforce no differently than they do spending on candy bars. According to these widely used statistics, a company is investing if it purchases a new machine but not if its pays for employee training on how to use that machine more efficiently.

The new paradigm sees employees for what they are: assets. Because it isn't possible to attach a number to all of the knowledge and skills of an employee doesn't mean that it isn't a critical company asset. Expenses related to employee training and development are capital investments that will bring a return as much as any other capital expenditure. In the new paradigm, company management nurtures and protects that investment, expecting to harvest abundant returns.

Management Is Personally Responsible for Commitments and Performance

Perhaps another way to say this is, "No more abandoned empires." Company managers make commitments on the behalf of the company every day—commitments that sometimes live on after the manager has moved to another position. Some managers give their careers a boost by making large commitments and building an empire of employees to fulfill that commitment. Unfortunately, many of these managers are concerned only about the short-term success of these commitments. They know that if they appear successful over the next couple of years, their track record will be good for a promotion. If it fails after sufficient time, it is certain that corporate attention will have moved elsewhere, and few people will remember the grand, and now unfulfilled, promises they made.

Under the new paradigm, company managers are held personally responsible for their commitments and the performance of those commitments. When a manager promises success and spends company funds pursuing it, he or she is held responsible for attaining these goals. If the newer, larger department is supposed to be cheaper than farming work out, the manager is held responsible for realizing those savings. If a greatly expanded sales force will increase sales, the manager is expected to deliver those increases.

Management accountability has long been held in high esteem, but it is not always practiced, especially in today's constantly changing business environment, where yesterday's promises are lost in the dust of repeated reorganizations and market changes. In many corporate environments, a manager need worry about a new program delivering results for only a year or eighteen months. If the program shows positive results in that time period, it is declared a success and the manager awarded kudos. After that time period, there is often a disconnection between the program failure and the manager's personal performance record. This failure is blamed on many factors but rarely chalked up to an ill-conceived, unplanned, and mismanaged project.

Reinvesting Profits in the Business Is Not "Anti-Shareholder" Activity

Increasingly, shareholders have been making demands on companies: that company management take responsibility for company performance, that companies be environmentally safe, and that a company articulate a long-term strategy. The shareholder voice, long silenced by the control of management, is gaining influence over the way many companies are run. Increasingly, some shareholder groups are demanding that companies pay them dividends regardless of company performance.

Especially during tough times, senior managers are eager to appease shareholders—shareholders who hold the reins of management careers. There is a strong push for even a marginally profitable company to pay a sizable dividend to investors, forcing some of these companies into the red. For many of these companies, slim profits, reinvested in the business, can make the difference between future stability or slow demise. The reinvestment of profit during times of restructuring can bring shareholders a much greater return in the long run. Under the new paradigm, shareholders must be willing to sacrifice a quick dividend for a long-term return on investment.

Reductions in Cost Should Be Focused and Always Coupled with Growth Strategies

Across-the-board cuts of a predetermined percentage make little sense to anyone but the company bookkeeper. No company that has remained in business has problems in every department across the organization. Cuts must be stratified to fit the problem, not simply to reduce expenses.

Not only should cuts be targeted to problem areas, but they should always be coupled with a strong plan for correcting the originating problem. If heavy research and development costs are the problem, what will be done in the future to keep the ideas flowing at a lower cost? Simply cutting the R&D budget won't do a thing for supporting the research function. As jobs in one department go away, there must be strategies for redeploying those company assets in other needed areas rather than wasting them by throwing them away.

Shedding the Reductionist Mentality

Compaq is widely touted as a downsizing success story and illustrates the operation of these two paradigms and how they affect company performance. During 1990–1991, Compaq began suffering from declining sales and profits after having been one of the most profitable makers of high-end personal computers during the 1980s. Compaq's board of directors became so alarmed that it fired founder Joseph ("Rod") Canion as chief executive and replaced him with Eckhard Pfeiffer, a former salesman. One of Pfeiffer's first acts as CEO was to fire 20 percent of the company's staff—nearly 9,000 workers.

Simultaneously with the layoff, Pfieffer moved the company from a maker of expensive, high-end computers to a mass producer of much less expensive personal computers. The result? Profits increased from $131 million in 1991 to $462 million in 1993 and an amazing $423 million just the first half of 1994. Sales have increased steadily, making Compaq the third largest computer manufacturer, with increases in market share continuing.

On the surface, Compaq might appear to be a trophy of the corporate reductionist philosophy—but only if you ignore one small fact. Within a year of firing those 9,000 workers, Compaq had hired more than 14,000 new employees. By its own admission, Compaq's strategy for growth worked so well that it had to "undo" the previous layoff. Had Compaq executed only that flawed plan for reduction, as so many companies do, it would have missed the monumental growth that came from creatively rethinking its business growth strategy. Luckily for Compaq's management, investors, and employees, company management was able to rise above the reductionist paradigm and see a new way of managing the business.

Another company that is adopting the new paradigm is United Airlines. Three months after taking over as chairman in 1994, Gerald Greenwald announced a strategy focusing on worker empowerment to help contain costs and boost profits. Greenwald began by making changes that will allow employees to make decisions in the company's best interest. For example, he has given pilots more freedom to set airspeed, a change that helped the airline report the best on-time performance in its history. He has rescinded some of the rules that have long been sore spots for United employees. Flight attendant weight limits have been relaxed, and prohibitions against wearing open-toed shoes have been lifted. Although it is much too soon to measure Greenwald's success, United's passenger loads are up, and analysts are positive regarding the company's financial outlook.

One former Sara Lee Corp. vice president, Jerry Kemp, took matters into his own hands. When Sara Lee announced it was closing the Cartersville factory of Spring City Knitting, a Winston-Salem, North Carolina, subsidiary, and laying off all 230 workers, Kemp resigned his position and along with three partners purchased the factory. After creative financing and retooling, the factory is churning out trendy undergarments. Most of the jobs have been saved, and the company is expecting to turn a profit in the next year. One company's liability under a reductionist paradigm was another's opportunity.

   Shedding the reductionist mentality is critical to the future success of American business. Corporate management must shift focus from the shortsighted goals of downsizing to the long-term strategies of growth and expansion. As the editor of *Business Week* put it, "What is the antidote to this bloodletting? Growth, growth and more growth."

15
A New Social Contract

One thing is painfully clear from the entire employment picture: Whether the worker is a layoff victim jumping from job to job or a layoff survivor hanging on to a precious paycheck, life in the workplace for all Americans—management and nonmanagement, blue collar or white collar—is deteriorating. Everyone seems to be losing ground at an alarmingly fast pace.

Decade of Erosion

The eighties and the early nineties were, by all measures, the age of revitalized materialism. During those years Americans reached a level of consumerism that had not existed since the roaring twenties. The popular culture icons of the time—everything from Madonna's "material girl" to *Dynasty*—reeked of conspicuous consumption. But while American workers were out shopping, out raising the limits of consumer debit, something sinister was brewing at the office. Workers began losing ground on many of the issues they had been fighting to improve since the 1920s. The losses at work are more than just a hangover from the overindulgences of the eighties; they add up to the harsh reality of a severely diminished livelihood. Now not only does the worker struggle to repay the debit of overspending, but he does so with less income than before.

American workers are slowly being robbed of their standard of living, health care, retirement income, leisure time, job security, and job satisfaction. Their jobs have become economic quicksand, sucking more of their time and energy and paying less in return. For the most part, these workers went to college, prepared for a career, and sought a "good" job with a "sound" company that would ensure well-being and secure their future. Sure, they expected to work hard and even sacrifice for the company, but one day the company would ante up for these years of sweat and loyalty. This dream has crumbled.

Over the past decade, America has witnessed an alarming erosion of the workplace. Numerous layoffs have added significantly to the workload and increased the stress level to an all-time high. With more to do, Americans work more hours than ever before, trying to stay ahead of the ax. Those marvelous inventions of the fax machine and cellular phone have made them completely accessible to work at any time or place. Perhaps the most alarming change is the real decline in the paycheck.

The Disappearing Paycheck

According to the Economic Policy Institute, the average white-collar income fell 4.4 percent between 1987 and 1991 after adjusting for inflation. Even *Fortune* magazine noted that for all workers, wages have decreased 1.5 percent over the past two decades. (The *Fortune* figure is conservative; it includes the enormous bonuses paid to senior managers since 1990.) To add insult to injury, what has appeared to be a shrinking of the gap between men and women's pay is due primarily to the falling income of men rather than rising pay for women during the eighties and early nineties.

Increased Hours

Hours and demands have increased to the highest levels of this century. According to economist Juliet Schor, author of *The Overworked American*, the average worker is on the job an additional 163 hours today as compared to 1969 (the equivalent of an extra month per year). Breaking that figure down, in 1969 the average workweek was 39.8 hours; in 1987 it was 40.7. Since 1987, that figure rose by 2.5 percent each year to 1994, when it jumped 3.6 percent.

Once source of increased working hours lies in the loss of paid vacation time: three and a half fewer days each year. This decline is in contrast to the increasing vacation time of Europeans, who have almost five weeks a year, and reverses a forty-year-old fight to increase paid time off. Another source of the increased working hours comes from workers who are refusing to stay at home when they are ill. According to James E. Challenger, of Challenger, Gray & Christmas, an international employment consulting firm, "Managers prefer to have people in the office, even if they are sick. . . . Everyone is working much harder than they have in years."

We have become a nation of workaholics. Perhaps we are seeking to keep up with the Joneses, an ever more difficult job, or to cover the work of our laid-off colleagues. Maybe we are bowing to the demands of corporate executives determined to squeeze more from less. Whatever the reason, a full one-fourth of us who have full-time jobs spend 49 or more hours on the job each week and, of those, almost half work 60 or more hours. When you couple this with an average commute time of 7 hours a week (more in urban areas or for those working on weekends), we spend the majority of our waking hours in work-related activities.

Increase in Job-Related Stress

It is no wonder that we are paying an enormous price for this schedule in stress. American workers report that they are under more stress today than they were five years ago. Of all visits to a primary care physician, 75 to 90 percent are stress related. A National Center for Health Statistics study of 40,000 workers found that more than half reported feeling either a lot or a moderate amount of stress during just the preceding two weeks, citing work-related problems as the major source. In real terms, this translates into 550 million workdays lost to stress-related absenteeism and a fiscal cost of $200 billion annually. As the demands grow, we are showing the wear for trying to keep our job.

Decrease in Job Satisfaction

With stress up and pay down, 63 percent of workers report that the workplace has lost its luster. They enjoy work less, gain less satisfaction from a job completed, and mistrust management more. The number one cause cited is "a dog-eat-dog environment," void of teamwork or cooperation. Oppressive and highly competitive, the workplace, where we spend the majority of our time, has become devoid of enjoyment and satisfaction.

A Roper survey in the mid-eighties found that 35 percent of all workers found their company less than a favorable place to work; in 1990 that figure had risen to 45 percent. In that same survey, only 43 percent said that their employer treated them with any respect.

Crowded Labor Market

Workers are chained to their job. With an abundant supply of unemployed and underemployed workers eager to find jobs, no one is in a position to deny a system that asks for more and pays less. The labor market is filled with laid-off middle managers and college graduates, many with graduate degrees, who are inundating employers with their resumés. These workers are often willing to work for less just to get a foot in the door. So who dares ask for a raise?

Although as of this writing, the job market shows some improvement, all bets are that it isn't going to rebound in this mid-1990s recovery as it has in the past. The Fortune 500 industrial companies employed 4.1 million fewer workers in 1994 than they did in 1981, for a loss of one in four jobs. The jobs that were lost belonged primarily to the larger companies and were relatively high paying. Of the new jobs that were created, roughly one-third of them paid less than $13,000, below poverty level for a family of four. The experts almost all agree that this trend will continue through the turn of the century, giving little hope of a quick turnaround.

Mistrust of Top Management

Something is desperately wrong. With newly hired college graduates now making 3.1 percent less than in 1987 and struggling to keep their increasingly stressful jobs and diminishing paychecks, it is no wonder that more than half of the white-collar workers in a national survey say they don't trust top management. How could they? The company house organs broadcast the necessity of cutbacks and concessions while top executives haul their loot out by the wheelbarrows.

Most employees were raised on the American dream and a strong work ethic. They believe that hard work, smart decisions, and tenacity in the face of difficulty deserve reward and prospertiy. They worked—they planned—they conformed—they sacrificed—and now they are losing. Change must happen. Change must bring relief.

A View From the Top

Just in case you're thinking that corporate management is enjoying a walk in the park while the workers keep their nose to the grindstone, look again. Corporate management has its own harrowing challenges with which to deal. Companies are being pushed for more efficiency, more productivity, more profit, and more dividends—all in a global market that isn't even close to a level playing field. Large corporations in other countries can often hire workers at a fraction of what it costs to hire Americans and work them longer hours in factories that cost far less than they would in the United States. To top it all off, some of these companies even enjoy subsidies from their governments, allowing them to produce goods and services at virtually unbeatable prices.

Of all the difficulties corporate America faces, probably the most frustrating and paradoxical is illustrated by what happened to maverick ice cream maker Ben & Jerry. In December 1994, Ben & Jerry, after having ten years of very profitable business, recorded its first quarterly loss. The loss, which came about because of a delay in opening a new, more efficient manufacturing plant, sent the company's stock price down 15 percent, in spite of the fact that the company expected to record a profit for the entire year. One San Francisco investment banker, Lewis H. Alton, told the Associated Press on December 20, 1994, "We think they were taken by their own success. We don't really see much lack of success, only success beyond which it could not compete." Like Ben & Jerry, other companies too are forced to compete with their own past successes. If revenues are not better than a previous year's revenues, Wall Street says the organization is faltering. Investors withdraw, creating real problems for company finances. The bottom line is that if you have a good year, you better have a plan to have an equally good or better one next year.

Amid these pressures, company management increasingly is turning to workers to help make the difference. Work smarter, harder, better, and faster. Speed up the cycle time, use total quality, work in teams for efficiency, manage your time, and take responsibility for your own health care and retirement. This is a no-win situation, and it has created unempowered victims out of workers and needless devils out of management. If there is anything that everyone in corporate America agrees on, it is that something must change.

A New Social Contract

Significant changes must occur in the social contract between employer and employee. The new contract must be workable for both sides. The corporate world isn't what it was in the 1940s and 1950s, when the current social contract flourished. Promises of job security, ongoing salary, and hierarchical careers inhibit companies from flowing and changing with the demands of the market.

Workers, on the other hand, must reap the rewards of their labor. They must be compensated fairly for their work. Health care, disability insurance, and retirement income must be provided through some means. Since employees must stay current with changing technology, reasonable opportunities for self-improvement must be provided. A workplace designed to foster innovation and satisfaction is essential to the well-being of workers and the future success of companies.

A new contract must allow workers the opportunity to prosper and provide employers with an adequate labor pool and the staffing flexibility they need to succeed. Such a contract would radically change the look of the workplace. The mounting frustration on both sides demands just such an agreement.

The New Employee

The new contract must create a new class of employees; I call them PIC (professional, independent contract) employees. This new army of working professionals will offer their services to the corporation for a specified period or project. Much like today's corporate consultants, they will offer their services for a fee that is directly tied to the delivery of a product. They are independent and are responsible for their own income, benefits, development, and retirement. PIC employees may work on-site for one company or work from their home or personal office for several companies, thanks to advances in communications technology (fax machines, computer modems, conference calls, and others).

The PIC employee sounds very much like what is now being called the temporary or contingent employee, but there is one very important distinction: The PIC employee will charge fees that are considerably higher than today's compensation structures for permanent employees (current temporary employees are usually paid the same rate as permanent employees but without benefits), for these reasons:

- PIC employees are responsible for their own health care, life insurance, and retirement plans. Fees must allow them to cover these expenses.
- PIC employees are obligated to keep their skills at the highest level if they hope to continue to get work. They alone are responsible for their own professional development.
- PIC employees assume responsibility to meet deadlines.
- PIC employees must spend some time marketing themselves between jobs to other companies. This is not billable time, and their fees must cover this marketing expense.

It is not enough for PICs simply to show up on time or to blame other circumstances for missed deadlines; they are paid to produce according to the agreements and timetables in the consulting contract.

PIC employees can obtain benefits from professional organizations rather than through a specific employer. These organizations offer group plans for health, retirement, and disability for those who are self-employed. As the ranks of PIC employees grow, more of these organizations can offer plans at rates that are comparable to what many pay now through a full-time employer. Under this system, employees can work for many employers over a career and not lose benefits with each move.

But what about company loyalty? Doesn't a contractual employee have less commitment to his or her employer? Not necessarily. Two people working together under a limited contract can be just as protective and loyal to one another as can an employee and employer. The fact is, employee loyalty isn't purchased. Loyalty is a function of reciprocity between two parties who have a mutual trust and respect. How much trust is there between an employee who receives a regular paycheck and an employer who is actively laying off other employees? In most cases there is very little. A paycheck buys regular attendance and productivity, but not loyalty. Loyalty is a product of a mutual respect—something the PIC employee is more likely to experience than today's permanent employee who lives under the continuous threat of being laid off.

Contractual employment is nothing new. Building contractors and craftsmen have used it for well over a century. Carpenters and painters, among others, agree to do a specific job for a contractor, who pays them by the hour or the job and supervises all of the work. If a carpenter does good work and does it quickly, the contractor may use that carpenter for many jobs. The carpenter, in return, gains satisfaction and reward for the quality and efficiency of his or her labor. All in all, both are responsible, both have choices, and, except under unusual circumstances, neither can blame the other for successes or failures.

The new contract will create changes in the corporation that will extend into every facet of the business. Everything from the organization chart to the steel and glass temples where they work will look entirely different. Changing the corporation from a roster of employees to a loosely connected network of contract professionals will dramatically shrink the size in number of employees and space of today's corporation. With this shrinking will come a shift in responsibility from the shoulders of the corporation to the workers. No longer will the company bear the time-consuming, parental responsibility for providing the material needs of its workers; nor will it be required to police their day-to-day activities. Instead, the company can focus time and attention on essential business strategy.

The New Manager

The job of managers under this new contract will finally become the professional manager long sought after by management consultants and business schools. Managers will spend far less than the 30 percent of their time now spent managing employees: performance reviews, vacations, sick leaves, expense reports, and the like. Now they will truly be responsible for a function, not for a group of employees. For example, a manager in charge of buying men's socks for a department store chain will no longer manage the comings and goings, hiring and firing of several buyers who gather information on socks at market and seek his approval on purchasing decisions. Instead, he will manage a number of specific contracts with professionals who may buy socks for any number of other stores. He can then focus his time on the more strategic tasks of evaluating the performance of different lines of socks and planning for future purchases. The new contract takes his attention off the non-business-related issues and gives more time to the actual business at hand.

This new role will demand greatly increased communications. Because the company will be more loosely connected, managers will have to take on the role of keeping all PIC employees in the network up to date on how the business is doing. There will be fewer opportunities to pass information along in the hallway, at the water cooler, or even at staff meetings. Using the tremendous advances in communications technology and group software, managers will keep all parts of the network informed and on track.

Workers stand to gain enormously under such a contract. This new contract will reward those who find ways to improve quality and work processes. Using the sock buyer example, if the employee learns how to use a personal computer to streamline purchasing decisions, then she reduces the amount of her time required but can continue billing the same amount. The new contract pushes down profits and provides powerful incentives to the worker to learn new and better ways of doing business. Coupled with these benefits is also the loss of victimization. No longer will the worker be able to place the entire blame for her situation on the company. As she becomes more in control of her own work, she has less reason to be victimized by the company.

Management, for its part, is removed from its adversarial, parental role. Company management need only carry responsibility for the skeleton of permanent staff. It is true that management is giving up some control along with that responsibility, but this very same control is a constant sticking point under the current social contract. Under the new contract, control by management is transformed into informed choice for the employees.

The New Organization

The new social contract between workers and the company will create a new kind of organization—one that Charles Handy in *The Age of Unreason* calls the shamrock organization. The three leaves of the shamrock represent each of the three distinct components of the new organization. The first leaf represents the professional core—the workers who are essential to the organization. They are employed full-time and form the core of organizational learning and control systems. They hold the organizational knowledge; without them, there is no organization. This leaf of Handy's shamrock is closest to today's full-time, permanent employee.

The second leaf represents smaller, specialized organizations to which the larger organization contracts much of its work. Because these smaller organizations specialize in limited endeavors, they can presumably do these tasks with greater speed and quality. This leaf of the shamrock organization is already employed to a large extent by many organizations. In fact, some organizations calculate that 80 pecent of the value of their product or service is provided by someone not inside their organization. The contractual fringe surrounding most organizations has become so large as to equal in size the organization itself. Under the new contract, this trend will continue.

Handy's third leaf of the shamrock is a flexible labor force—the PIC employees. Airports and airlines are busier in the summer. Retail shops are busier during holidays and sale periods. Plant nurseries thrive on weekends, especially in the spring. Defense contractors are far busier when they have contracts then when they don't. By using PIC employees, organizations can hire the expertise they need when they need it. This flexible labor force may be part of many organizations at any given time, depending on the demand for their services.

A Call for Change

Until workers and companies alike are willing to abandon a social contract that is choking each out of a decent livelihood, American business will be unable to escape the insanity of the layoff craze. Companies will still hire with false implications of continued employment and lay off those same employees when the demand for work subsides. Workers will continue to lose salary and benefits as organizations find the liability of payroll too great to bear. Companies struggling for existence in a world of heated competition and angry shareholders will continue to push workers for more yet offer less in return.

Ultimately we much change our fundamental beliefs about workplace roles. Expectations that were forged in the early days of this century aren't possible in today's business. Pensions, health care, and salary cannot be doled out and controlled by corporations, as they have been through the past seventy-plus years. The majority of workers must come to see themselves as mobile and as having a portfolio of work that they manage for many organizations rather than working for a single employer-provider.

The success of American business hinges on this change. Without it, a reasonable solution—one that treats workers with dignity and humanity—isn't possible. The torturous cycle of layoffs will continue to spin out of control, devastating more individuals, families, and communities. We must reach to a higher ideal that values profit and the livelihood of corporate citizens. By discarding the old social contract and replacing it with the new, we can achieve both objectives. The workforce and the company will thrive equally in a world where change and technological advancement will continue to race forward. By changing the way we view our roles and the structure of organizations to accommodate the new roles, we can equip ourselves to survive and prosper from whatever change the future brings.

Notes on Sources

Chapter 1

Page

4 **WESTINGHOUSE REPORTS FIRST PROFIT:** *Pittsburgh Post-Gazette* (January 25, 1995).

4 **"an operational hedge":** Rick Gladstone, "Despite the Strong Numbers, There Were Rude Awakenings," Associated Press (December 21, 1994).

11 **A survey of 1,005 corporations:** Frank Lalli, "Learn From My Mistake," *Money* (February 1992), p. 5.

13 **Dow Chemical estimates that the cost:** Edmund Faltermayer, "Is This Layoff Necessary?" *Fortune* (June 1, 1992), p. 71.

14 **"The typical upturn":** Robert Reich, "Of Butchers and Bakers," *Vital Speeches* (October 8, 1993), p. 100.

20 **"layoffs are horribly expensive":** Edmund Faltermayer, "Is This Layoff Necessary?" *Fortune* (June 1, 1992), p. 71.

Chapter 2

22 **It's a sin to lose money:** "Crosscurrents: Rewards for Layoffs," *At Work* (March/April 1994), p. 20.

23 **one senior manager described:** "The Attack of the Killer Boards," *Esquire* (April 1993), pp. 80–81.

23 **Carl Icahn, CEO of TWA:** "His Money, Carl Icahn Plays the Tough Guy," *Philadelphia Inquirer* (March 27, 1986), p. A19.

28 **in 1993 the average senior executive's stock:** Brian Du-
    maine, "A Knckout Year for CEO Pay," *Fortune* (July 25,
    1994), p. 103.

30 **The board raised the dividend:** Mike McKesson,
    "Chrysler Pleases Top Shareholder," *New Orleans Times-
    Picayune* (December 1, 1994).

32 **"sentimentally demented":** Richard Cohen, "Profits Be-
    fore People: Do Companies Have Any Obligation to Work-
    ers?" *Washington Post* (August 19, 1993).

33 **"It's an American company":** "Japan's Stuggle to Restruc-
    ture," *Fortune* (June 28, 1992).

34 **In fact, there are many economists:** "In a Downturn, Cut
    Profits Before Jobs," *New York Times* (February 16, 1992).

35 **Astrid Molder, a public relations employee:** Nathaniel
    Nash, "Waking an Old East German Giant," *New York
    Times* (December 2, 1994).

36 **In a *Business Week* article:** John A. Byrne, "He's Gutsy,
    Brilliant, and Carries an Ax," *Business Week* (May 9, 1994).

37 **Graef Crystal, a well-known compensation consultant:**
    David McNaughton, "Goizueta Ranked Among 'Over-
    paid' CEOs," Cox News Service (November 30, 1994).

37 **One brave consultant:** Frank A. Petro, "Why Layoffs Don't
    Work," *San Francisco Chronicle* (March 18, 1994).

38 **Analyst Brenda Lee of Morgan Stanley:** Ben Dobbin,
    "Eastman Kodak Pares Down Even More Under New
    Boss," Associated Press (November 30, 1994).

Chapter 3

42 **Not all layoff-inspired sabotage:** Ernest Brod, "In the Lay-
    off Era, the 'Get Even' Ethic," *New York Times* (January 26,
    1992), p. F-13.

45 **When the *Chicago Tribune* expanded:** Profits Up, Spirits
    Down," *Chicago Tribune* (January 12, 1993).

45 **A 1994 Conference Board study:** "Change Management:
    An Overview of Current Initiatives," The Conference
    Board (June 15, 1994).

46 **C. K. Prahalad, a professor:** "Xerox Tries to Duplicate Quality Amid Layoffs," *Sales & Marketing Management* (February 1994), p. 14.

47 **One of the most terrifying:** "Nurses Say Patients Feeling the Pain of Staffing Cutbacks," *Boston Globe* (October 31, 1994), section 3, p. 37.

47 **"They've continually pushed themselves":** Christopher Connell, "Replacement of RNs Lowering Patient Care, Nurses Say," Associated Press (February 8, 1995).

49 **The layoff rocked the counterculture:** "Too Good to Be True," *Inc.* (July 1994).

51 **Adam Zak, a recruiter from Chicago:** Lee Smith, "Burned-Out Bosses: The other victims of restructuring," *Fortune* (July 25, 1994), p. 44.

53 **One of the most popular managing-survivors booklets:** Price Prichett and Ron Pound, *Business as Unusual* (Dallas: Prichett Publishing Company, 1988).

Chapter 4

59 **At the first Caddo Parish Commission meeting:** Brad Cooper, "AT&T Seeks $1 Million Tax Break," *Shreveport Times* (November 9, 1993).

62 **According to Joliet's third-generation merchant:** Ronald Yates, "Joliet—Rough Passage: It's Had Tough Times, But City Harbors Hope It's on Right Course," *Chicago Tribune* (January 4, 1993).

63 **"The river boat owners":** Mitchell Zuckoff, "Riverboat City Finds Boon, Bane in Casinos," *Boston Globe* (October 9, 1994), p. 1.

64 **John D. Bamford:** Elizabeth Rau, "Many in R.I. Are Living in Poverty for First Time," *Providence Journal-Bulletin* (October 27, 1991).

65 **The state budget director:** Barbara A. Serrano and Jim Simon, "Boeing Cuts to Hit State Taxpayers," *Seattle Times* (January 27, 1993).

Chapter 10

127 **If I were going to weep:** Mary Rowland, "The Plight of the Middle Manager," *New York Times* (December 16, 1994).

132 **One snapshot of how many older workers:** "Caught Up in Downsizing," American Association for Retired Persons, 1994.

133 **Scott Bass, a gerontologist:** "Workplace Age Bias Rising, But Proving It Can be a Job," *Boston Globe* (January 31, 1994), sec. 3, p. 25.

134 **In Massachusetts, age discrimmination complaints:** Ibid.

134 **According to Martin Sicker:** Robert Lewis, "Downsizing Taking a Higher Toll," *AARP Bulletin* (November 1994).

135 **In 1994, Lotus was sued:** "Lotus Executives Defend Company Against Accusations of Age Discrimination," *Boston Globe* (November 10, 1994).

136 **A Toyota spokesperson said this move:** "Toyota Sets Age Limits for Managers," *New York Times* (October 25, 1994).

137 **One corporate raider, Victor Posner:** Donald L. Barlett and James B. Steele, *America: What Went Wrong?* (Kansas City: Andrews & McMeel, 1992).

Chapter 11

141 **How many of these statements:** "Cutting Your Losses," *New Orleans Times-Picayune* (November 18, 1994), p. C1.

146 **Professional outplacement consultants have typically said:** Richard L. Knowdell, Elizabeth Branstead, and Milan Moravec, *From Downsizing to Recovery* (Palo Alto, Calif.: Consulting Psychologist Press, 1994).

Chapter 12

155 **there is no documented evidence:** Ibid.

156 **By not giving employees information:** "Too Good to be True," *Inc.* (July 1994).

Chapter 13

163 **Right and Associates found:** "Lessons Learned: Dispelling the Myths of Downsizing," Right Associates (March 1992).

164 **According to BB&T chairman:** "BB&T, Southern National Announce That Attrition, Early-Out Program Will Reduce Layoffs," *PRNewswire* (November 18, 1994).

167 **Most companies, however, can expect:** Stuart Silverstein, "Want to Retire Early? Let Me Twist Your Arm," *Los Angeles Times* (November 28, 1992).

Chapter 14

191 **according to the latest Census Bureau analysis:** "Job Cutting Medicine Fails to Remedy Productivity Ills at Many Companies," *Wall Street Journal* (June 7, 1994).

193 **In February 1995, Geneva Overholser:** Tim Jones, "Top Editors Resign at Des Moines Register; Staff Cite Profit Pressure," *Chicago Tribune* (February 17, 1995).

194 **Henry Kelly and Andrew Wyckoff of the federal:** "Three New Ways to Create Jobs," *Atlantic Monthly* (July 28, 1994).

198 **As the editor of *Business Week:*** "Stay the Corporate Ax—With Growth," *Business Week* (May 9, 1994).

Chapter 15

200 **According to economist Juliet Schor:** Juliet B. Schor, *The Overworked American: The Unexpected Decline of Leisure* (New York: Basic Books, 1992).

201 **According to James E. Challenger:** Lisa Genasci, "Take Two Aspirins and Go to Work: On the Job Working Sick," Associated Press (February 15, 1995).

Suggested Readings

Barker, Joel Arthur. *Paradigms: The Business of Discovering the Future.* New York: William Morrow, 1992.

Hakim, Cliff. *We Are All Self-Employed.* San Francisco: Berrett Koehler, 1994.

————. *When You Lose Your Job.* San Francisco: Berrett Koehler, 1993.

Handy, Charles. *The Age of Unreason.* Boston: Harvard Business School Press, 1990.

Knowdell, Richard L., E. Branstead, and M. Moravec. *From Downsizing to Recovery.* Palo Alto, Calif.: Consulting Psychologist Press, 1994.

Olmsted, Barney, and S. Smith. *Creating a Flexible Workplace: How to Select and Manage Alternative Work Options.* New York: AMACOM, 1994.

Rothwell, William J. *Effective Succession Planning: Ensuring Leadership Continuity and Building Talent from Within.* New York: AMACOM, 1994.

Index